BOSTON BORO

The
EAST LINCOLNSHIRE RAILWAY

by
A.J. Ludlam

Market Place, Louth

THE OAKWOOD PRESS

© Oakwood Press 1991

ISBN 0 85361 416 4

Typeset by Gem Publishing Company, Brightwell, Wallingford, Oxfordshire.

Printed in Great Britain by The Nuffield Press Limited, Cowley, Oxford.

For John and Iris, my parents.

A view of the northern end of Alford station showing the signal box and crossing in
the early 1900s.   *Author's Collection*

Published by
The OAKWOOD PRESS
P.O.Box 122, Headington, Oxford.

Contents

A delightful rural scene: signalman Turner outside his box at Highferry in August 1935. A fine display of geraniums is in evidence inside the box. *Alan Turner*

A beautiful scene at the southern end of Alford Town station in GNR days showing the overall roof. The southbound train of six-wheelers is drawn by a GNR 2–2–2 engine, No. 266. Built by Sturrock as a class '264', No. 266 was rebuilt by Stirling in 1873 and withdrawn in

Introduction

Greyly tremendous the thunder
Hung over the width of the wold
But here the green marsh was alight
In a huge cloud cavern of gold,
And there, on a gentle eminence,
Topping some ash trees, a tower
Silver and brown in the sunlight,
Worn by sea-wind and shower,
Lincolnshire Middle Pointed.

John Betjeman

Lincolnshire, more than any other county in England perhaps, has among its attractions certain natural features which, if not quite peculiar to itself, blend with each other so harmoniously, or exist side by side in such striking contrasts, that aspects are presented which have their counterpart nowhere else. To appreciate the diverse characteristics of Lincolnshire and the appeal of their combined charms, it is necessary to acquaint oneself with the distinct attractiveness of each in order to delight in the subtle changes and surprises which unfold before the traveller.

Generally speaking the main natural features of Lincolnshire are its seashore, fens and wolds. To the newcomer they are a revelation of massive spaciousness, in places only comparable to the wide levels of Holland or the South American savannas in their apparent boundlessness, stretching away in every direction to a level horizon. It takes a long acquaintance to see beyond a casual impression of monotony and recognise their significance and experience their spectacular variability. On this stage great transformation scenes have taken place. Many years ago the sea covered great expanses, lapping shores that are now far inland beyond the sound of even the angriest sea.

The Lincolnshire Wolds run from Spilsby, in the south, to Barton-on-Humber, in the north. Contrasted with the level fens they assume the importance of really high hills. There is pleasant country, delightful scenery and clear bracing air.

Railway promoters became seriously interested in the untapped region of Lincolnshire in 1844. Several lines were proposed to link London with York, all passing through the county and some through Lincoln itself. The East Lincolnshire Railway (ELR), had strong links with the London and York proposals of 1844, sharing the services of two of its Directors, Edmund Denison and George Hussey Packe. The London and York changed its name to the Great Northern Railway (GNR), on 5th May, 1846. Its proposals threatened the traffic of all the established railways connecting London with the north for it offered a shorter and cheaper route.

Not included in the 39 Lincolnshire Bills offered to Parliament, but an amusing parady of the extent of railway mania, was a proposal for, 'The Bridge End, Burton Pedwardine, Scredington, Three Queens and Midland Junction Railway', to quote from an advertisement placed in the *Stamford Mercury*, by Messrs Bubble and Squeak of Scredington, and Timothy Teazer of Burton Pedwardine.

The 14 miles of railway between Louth and Grimsby formed the first route to be operated by the GNR. It was opened on 1st March, 1848, and trains were to run through to New Holland by virtue of an agreement with the Manchester, Sheffield and Lincolnshire Railway (MS&LR), the latter company also having running rights between Grimsby and Louth. The line south of Louth opened to Firsby on 3rd September and to Boston on 1st October, 1848, and the route through to Peterborough, a fortnight later. For the following 122 years the line proved to be a fast, direct link with London, enjoying, initially, main line, and later, secondary main line status.

My task is to deal with the history of the section between Boston and Grimsby promoted by the ELR company, worked by the GNR, but remaining in the control of the parent company until the 1923 Grouping. I have decided to concentrate my efforts on the history of the line as a complete unit, so effectively ending the story in 1970. However, reference will be made to the latter days of the Louth to Grimsby section which remained open for a further ten years, and the Skegness branch which is still working. It is also not my intention to write detailed histories of the railways of Boston and Grimsby; these are excellently dealt with elsewhere, and recommendations for further reading are made in the Acknowledgements. Instead I have tried to deal in some detail with the larger and more important stations along the line: Louth, Alford, Firsby and Willoughby.

The imposing entrance to the superb Louth station building showing a fine set of six horses possibly belonging to Captain Smythe of Elkington Hall.
D. N. Robinson Collection

Chapter One
Early Days

The enquiries of Mr Thomas Jackson, on behalf of the East Lincolnshire company, into the amount of traffic entering and leaving Louth in 1844, fully commended the promotion of a railway from Louth to Grimsby. Like all great innovative schemes it did find opposition among those whose own interests were best served by things remaining as they were; such opposition, predictably, presented itself when a railway was contemplated.

Fortunately, however, such opposition was in a minority and when the East Lincolnshire company announced its proposals on 16th April, 1845 under the heading, 'The East Lincolnshire Railway', it had the sanction of many 'Noblemen and Gentlemen Proprietors of land in, or otherwise connected with East Lincolnshire', including The Right Hon. the Earl of Yarborough, The Right Hon. Lord Willoughby d'Eresby, Lord Worsley (MP for North Lincolnshire), Lt Col Sir Edward Brackenbury, R.A. Christopher (MP for North Lincolnshire), Christopher Turner (MP for South Lincolnshire), Edward Heneage (MP for Great Grimsby), George Tomline (MP for Riby Grove), and the Mayor of Louth. A Committee of Direction included George Heneage, Richard Thorald, Charles Henry Mundy, Edmund Beckett Denison, Francis Mowatt, George Hussey Packe, Thomas Wetherell, Michael Ellison and James Wall. The Engineers were Messrs Joseph Gibbs and John Fowler. The company's prospectus read as follows:

This line of railway is projected for the purpose of establishing a communications by railway along the coast of an important maritime district, as of affording to the rich grazing and agricultural divisions of the county of Lincoln a more cheap and ready access to the London and Yorkshire markets and of completing the eastern chain of railway communications through this important county.

The advantages offered to the grazers and cattle feeders of that part of Lincolnshire which supplies both the London and Yorkshire markets with so large a portion of the fat stock and to the towns of Louth, Wainfleet, Spilsby and Alford by providing a more certain and ready transit for manufactured goods and articles of merchandise, cannot be estimated too highly.

The prospective districts around these towns will also fully participate in the advantages of this communication with the manufacturing and large consuming towns of Yorkshire to which nearly the entire produce of corn and wool from such districts is now transported by water carriage so tedious, expensive and uncertain of delivery as materially to depress the price of produce in the markets of these towns and to place such produce at great disadvantage as compared with that of other markets possessing great facilities of transit.

A very considerable return traffic in coal from the Yorkshire coalfields would be obtained and this article of absolute necessity, at present supplied to the population of this part of the country at an expense enormously increased by the difficulties of carriage, would be afforded at a greatly reduced price.

Independently of these local advantages it is impossible to overrate those of a more general and even national character connected with the projected improvements of the port of Great Grimsby, the locality of which, at the mouth of the Humber, affords facilities superior to any other port with reference to the Baltic and Hamburg trades, or the Mails between London and the northern continental ports.

In the article of fish alone, in the transit of which every hour's delay is of so much importance, it is calculated that a great proportion of the supply from the northern seas would necessarily be transmitted to the Metropolis through this line.

The line has also the important advantage of the cordial approval and support of the principal landed proprietors through whose estates it will pass.

The county is peculiarly favourable, and the cheap construction and excellent gradients of the line will permit its being worked as far as cost as cheaply as any in the kingdom.

The Committee of Direction have authority to increase or reduce the capital and generally to adopt such measures as they may think for obtaining the requisite Parliamentary powers to form a company for the construction of the entire railway, or any portion thereof, with such branchlines and extensions as they may hereafter find expedient, and to apply the deposits in discharge of any liabilities which they may incur under the general powers vested in them for the prosecution of the undertaking.

Application for shares to be made to the solicitors on or before the 30th inst. Thomas Reynolds, 7 Lothbury, April 21st, 1845

Originally the East Lincolnshire had intended to terminate its line off the High Street in Boston on the west bank of the Haven by Pulvertoft Lane. The London and York (later GNR) had proposed that its station would be situated in the Skirbeck Quarter. Boston Corporation took great exception to both proposals. Eventually both companies agreed to cross West Street to the west of the Queens Street junction on a common line and share the temporary station north of the West Street level crossing.

In Grimsby it was intended to run into Pasture Street, however agreement was reached with the MS&LR for East Lincolnshire trains to run into Grimsby station, this was effected by means of a sharp curve extending from Catherine Street to Garden Street. Both the East Lincolnshire and the Great Northern Railway Bills were given Royal Assent on 26th June, 1846.

A print of the impressive and elegant Louth station, published by J. W. Wallis, of Upgate, Louth, in February 1848.   *D. N. Robinson Collection*

Chapter Two
Construction of the Line

In January 1847, great preparations were being made in a field on Brackenborough Road, Louth, through which the line would pass. The field was full of piles of timber and up to 70 labourers were engaged in making several sawpits and a large shed for the reception of a steam engine. This was to be used to provide power for sawing wood which would be converted into hurdles by which the line was to be continuously fenced off.

It was anticipated that work on the construction of the line would be accomplished quickly, indeed at a meeting of the company in May 1847, at its offices, 36, George Street, Westminster, George Hussey Packe suggested that the 14 miles between Louth and Grimsby would be opened before the end of July that year. With an estimated expenditure of under £9,000 a mile for the double line of rails and because of the nature of the country the railway passed through, expectations were formed regarding its likely profitability. However, the contractor's practice of working his men on Sundays did not find favour with the *Lincolnshire Chronicle*, which on 30th April, 1847 reported:

> The works on the line are rapidly progressing. We understand that rather early on Sunday morning last, several workmen were actually engaged in the lordship of Ludborough in putting down temporary rails, a circumstance much regretted, reflecting as it does, on the morals of the contractors and indeed truly disgraceful to our profoundly enlightened nation.

The attack continued on 4th June:

> We regret that it is our painful duty to report that on Sunday last workmen were employed on the line running through Fotherby. We look upon this as a gross violation of the Sabbath, as not only being disgraceful to the contractor's of the works and the operators of the line, but England as a nation and we sincerely hope for the well-being of our country, that steps will be promptly taken to the extent of our existing law to prevent so painful a repetition.

A week later the newspaper's outrage was vindicated when local magistrates fined some of the offending workmen.

At a meeting of the company at the end of May it was reported that three Bills promoted by the company had passed the committee stage and had been reported to the House of Commons. The first was to authorise a deviation of the ELR at Boston and the construction of a branch to join the Manchester, Sheffield and Lincolnshire line near Grimsby; the second was to authorise the ELR to purchase the remainder of a lease of the Louth Navigation, and the third was to enable the GNR to lease or purchase the East Lincolnshire line. The Bills were unanimously approved and the common seal of the company attached thereto. The Chairman also explained that the Directors had been authorised to prosecute a Bill for the construction of a branch railway to connect Louth with Lincoln. This Bill had been withdrawn because a satisfactory alternative arrangement had been effected with the MS&LR.

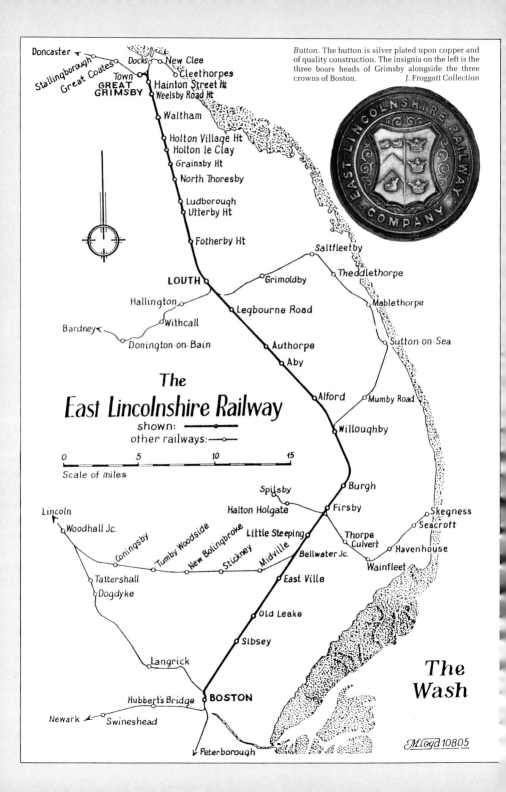

Doncaster
Stallingborough
Great Coates
Docks
Town
GREAT
GRIMSBY
New Clee
Cleethorpes
Hainton Street Ht
Weelsby Road Ht
Waltham
Holton Village Ht
Holton le Clay
Grainsby Ht
North Thoresby
Ludborough
Utterby Ht
Fotherby Ht

Button. The button is silver plated upon copper and of quality construction. The insignia on the left is the three boars heads of Grimsby alongside the three crowns of Boston.   *J. Froggatt Collection*

Saltfleetby
Theddlethorpe
LOUTH
Grimoldby
Hallington
Leqbourne Road
Mablethorpe
Withcall
Bardney
Donington-on-Bain
Authorpe
Aby
Sutton-on-Sea

The
East Lincolnshire Railway
shown: ———
other railways: —o—

Alford
Mumby Road
Willoughby

0   5   10   15

Scale of miles

Burgh

Spilsby
Lincoln
Halton Holgate
Firsby
Skegness
Woodhall Jc.
Seacroft
Coningsby
Tumby Woodside
New Bolingbroke
Little Steeping
Thorpe Culvert
Havenhouse
Stickney
Midville
Bellwater Jc.
Wainfleet
Tattershall
East Ville
Dogdyke

Old Leake

Sibsey

Langrick

The
Wash

Hubbert's Bridge
BOSTON
Newark
Swineshead

Peterborough

McLoyd 10805

At the half-yearly meeting of the company held at the London Tavern, Bishopgate Street, in August, the company Secretary, reported that all three Bills had received Royal Assent, and that the Louth Navigation investment was already showing a good return and that its annual expectation exceeded that of some operating railways. In order to conform with their agreement, the GNR was to provide the stock and engines, carriages, wagons etc. for working the line as the various portions were opened. By virtue of an arrangement with that company and the MS&LR, the distance between Louth and the Humber ferries was to be worked as one line at the beginning. Each company was to receive its proportion of the receipts and to find, or give credit to the other, its proportion of the working stock.

Although events were progressing smoothly at executive level, there were still occasional problems within the localities through which the railway was being constructed. The ever observant *Lincolnshire Chronicle* reported on 21st May:

> On Saturday night last, being the conclusion of the annual feast held in the village of North Thoresby, a great number of farmers' servants from this and the adjacent villages, also a considerable influx of workmen upon the East Lincolnshire railway passing through the lordship, assembled in and about the Inn and continued drinking until a late hour, when a most fearful disturbance took place, which amounted to a serious affray. Two of the railway police were much injured, the mob having taken recourse to stakes and bludgeons etc. and fought most desperately, but no lives were lost, which, in all probability would have been the case, had not the large railings opposite the Inn prevented the parties falling into a great drain. The night being dark prevented the constabulary force recognising friend from foe in certain stages of the conflict.

In the same month, the ELR Directors advertised the availability of contracts for the erection of stations along the line. Plans were available from Mr Fowler's office in Abingdon Street, Westminster. The Directors were to meet on 27th May to receive the tenders and award the contract.

By the end of July the line was not open, as had earlier been predicted by George Hussey Packe but nevertheless good progress was reported at Louth and on the line itself: 'A steam engine is at work conveying soil from one part to another. The station at Louth promises to be an important building.'

On Friday, 17th September, some of the Directors and their friends travelled over the line. The train consisted of two GNR carriages, a second class and a third class, described as, 'of very superior finish and accomodation.' The train left Keddington Road gate house, at 2.02 pm, amid the streaming of flags and the cheers of thousands of onlookers attracted by the novelty of the event. Among those on the train were Mr Packe and Mr Thorold, Chairman and Vice-Chairman of the Directors of the ELR company; Major Chaplin, Mr Wetherell, Captain Laws, manager of the GNR; Benjamin Cubitt, presiding over the locomotive department and Joseph Cubitt, Chief Engineer to the GNR. The run was satisfactory and was made in 20 minutes, including stops. No oscillation was noticed in the carriages which was interpreted as a compliment to the high quality of the track. After a short stay in Grimsby, the train returned to Louth at about 5.30 pm, welcomed by cheering crowds and the ringing of the bells of the parish church there. By this time it was intended that the line would be open to the public by November, with an anticipated journey time of between 15 and 30 minutes. At the same time the third of Louth's bridges was being built by Thomas Pickering and commented upon most favourably:

> The arch will form a segment of a circle and from the specimen of workmanship supplied in the side walls and wings it is believed Mr Pickering will present as finished a piece of work of this kind as is anywhere to be met with. The three bridges, however, and the line to Boston cannot be made available to the public until next June, when the entire 48 miles of rail constituting the East Lincolnshire Railway, from Boston to Grimsby will most likely be opened.

By the beginning of October much building was taking place between Louth and Grimsby under the supervision of the chief clerk, Mr Cullen. At Fotherby, a gate house was already roofed and at Pear Tree Lane, Utterby, the floor of a gatehouse had been laid. At Ludborough the station was almost complete and North Thoresby was ready for its roof. The station houses at Holton-le-Clay and Waltham were just started and the gatehouse at Weelsby Lane, in Grimsby, was nearly finished and ready for roofing.

In November, an accident occurred involving 18 wagons, most of which were severely damaged. The accident happened when the wagons ran up against the temporary engine shed at North Thoresby, one of them breaking an axle, breaking and throwing the whole train off the line. The police and others on the engine escaped unhurt.

The *Stamford Mercury* announced on 21st January, 1848 that the line between Louth and Grimsby would be opened on 1st March:

> The carriages, built by Mr Williams of Goswell Road, are ready for delivery. A communication by the guard with the enginemen has been contrived which is as simple as it can be. It consists of a cord passing through a tube located along the upper part of the side of the several carriages of a train, from the guards compartment to the engine. It is intended that it shall be connected with the whistle or a bell. In order to prevent the slacking of the cord between the carriages, (where, of course, there is no tube), the cord is kept gently tightened by means of a spring, like the main-spring in a watch. The spring necessarilly is not sufficiently strong to pull the bell or blow the whistle when called into action by buffing. Between each carriage the cord can be disconnected and fastened by a simple contrivance in order that carriages may be added or taken away from the train.

Original stations on the Louth to Grimsby section of the line were at Ludborough, North Thoresby, Holton-le-Clay and Tetney, and Waltham and Humberston. A junction with the MS&LR docks line had been sanctioned by an Act of Parliament on 2nd July, 1847. This arrangement, however, entailed an inconvenient reversal in order to enter Grimsby Town Station. Shortly before the opening of the line it was decided to construct a sharp 20 chain curve to allow trains to run into the station, via Garden Street Junction. Parliamentary permission for the purchase of the necessary land was obtained retrospectively by an Act of 22nd July, 1848. The original connection with the docks line remained in place.

By 3rd September, 1848, the line reached Firsby (19 miles), stations being provided at Legbourne, Authorpe, Claythorpe, Alford, Willoughby and

EAST LINCOLNSHIRE RAILWAY.

THE Directors being of opinion that it is expedient to continue to prosecute this undertaking, desire to state that the following are their reasons:—

BECAUSE the Bill has passed every ordeal of the House of Commons, and now awaits in that House the *third* reading.

BECAUSE arrangements have been made to comply with the Standing Order of the House of Lords, requiring a 10 per Cent. deposit, and no calls will be made upon the Shareholders during the present year.

BECAUSE no opposition to the passage of the Bill through the House of Lords is anticipated, and therefore the Directors feel that the principal cost of the Act has been incurred.

BUT more especially because the Line of Railway is of a very favorable character; is much desired in the District, and offers every inducement for investment.

THOMAS REYNOLDS,

Secretary.

Offices—No. 4, CHARING CROSS,

London, 29th April, 1846.

Part of a statement issued by the Directors of The East Lincoln-shire Railway. April 1846.

THE GREAT NORTHERN & EAST LINCOLNSHIRE RAILWAYS.

SUPERINTENDENT'S OFFICE,

13th December, 1849.

Special Order.

DAMAGE TO CARRIAGES, WAGGONS, SHEETS, &c.

IT IS HEREBY ORDERED, that every Clerk in Charge, or Station Master, shall report to me without any delay, the name of the owners, number, description, and destination of every Carriage, Waggon, and Sheet, which arrives at, or leaves his Station, IN A DAMAGED STATE; with a particular account of the nature and extent of the injury, and how, and by whom caused; the number of the Train, and name of the Guard by which it arrived, and was despatched.

In event of an accident occurring, the Clerk in Charge of the nearest Station shall make to me a full and particular report of the cause and nature of the accident, the number of the Engine, names of the Driver, Fireman, and Guard; the owners, number, description, and destination of every Carriage or Waggon on the Train; and the extent of the injury done to each Carriage, or Waggon, and its contents.

Every damage to a Carriage, Waggon, or Sheet shall be charged to the Station to which it can be last traced, and from which no report of the injury has been received.

Special Order.

CATTLE WAGGONS.

After this date, Waggons with Sheep or Cattle are not on any account to be attached to the Passenger Trains, but are to be forwarded by Goods Trains; and Special Trains will be provided, when required, on application to Doncaster, Gainsborough, Lincoln, Boston, Louth, and Peterborough.

A directive issued by the GNR to station masters in December 1849.

Burgh. The final section from Firsby to Boston was completed by the end of September, with intermediate stations at Little Steeping, East Ville and New Leake, Hob Hole and Sibsey.

The line, double throughout, was constructed of 71 lb. rails in 15 ft lengths, resting on joint chairs of 31 lb. and intermediate chairs of 21 lb., secured to the sleepers by two wooden trenails. Signal posts and lamps were made by Stevens and Son of Darlington.

John Waring and Sons, of Howarth, near Rotherham, had contracted to build the line between Louth and Grimsby for a sum of £46,102, the contract being signed on 31st December, 1846. A further agreement between the East Lincolnshire company and John Waring for the construction of the line extending from Louth to Boston, at a cost of £123,000, was signed on 20th November, 1847. However, on 7th January, 1848, an indenture was issued releasing Waring and Sons from the second contract. This contract was fulfilled by Peto and Betts.

John Fowler, the Engineer, was contracted at £350 per mile, this price was quite specifically to include 'every expense belonging to the Engineer's department'.

The East Lincolnshire company's minutes note that in December, 1849, John Fowler's account totalled £19,151 8s. 4d. and that by 7th February, 1851, the balance had been paid to him.

An agreement of 1849 between the GNR and Thomas Edmondson of Salford, secured the use of his patent ticket apparatus, although the system had been in use on the ELR since the beginning; the licence cost 10s. per mile per annum. Edmondson printed and supplied the tickets at 3s. per thousand, plain backed and 3s. 3d. per thousand, initial backed, until the price was cut to 2s. per thousand, in August 1861, by Waterlow's who were the company's contractors for printing. Edmondson also supplied dating presses and ticket cases.

An LNER 4–4–0, class 'D4' locomotive at Boston in 1926. This engine was rebuilt to class 'D3' in 1928.   *J. E. Kite*

Chapter Three
Opening of the Louth–New Holland Railway

After describing Grimsby as 'a miserable collection of mean brick houses and ill painted streets', the *Railway Chronicle* in its 4th March, 1848 edition, pointed out that although convenient for the reception of ships from the Baltic, there was no market for produce, but, 'Railways will amend this', it suggested. The paper continued:

> In addition to the lines they [The Manchester, Sheffield and Lincolnshire Railway] have purchased at a moderate price the old dock of Grimsby, a long canal running up to the town with a water capacity of about 17 acres, and they have commenced the construction of a new dock from plans by Mr Rendel. One fact will give an idea of what Grimsby may expect to become. Five years ago the Customs receipts were £200 less than the expenses; in 1847 the clear profits over the expenses were £70,000.

The docks area was successively developed by the MS & LR, Great Central, the London and North Eastern, and British Railways. At its peak the area consisted of six docks with a total water area of 139 acres, a total length of quays of 6 miles and 81 miles of railway track.

On Tuesday 29th February, 1848 reported the *Railway Chronicle*,

> . . . a party of the Directors of the MS & LR, who are also proprietors of the ferry between Hull and New Holland, crossed from Hull in one of the new swift steamers they have lately purchased from a Gravesend company. The passage was effected in a quarter of an hour. At New Holland we first touched upon the works. A pier 1,500 ft in length extends into the water, and will not only enable passengers to embark and disembark at all times of the tide, but forms a continuation of the station and platform. It will be covered and lighted with gas, and the rails of the New Holland line will be continued to the extremity, so that passengers to and from Hull will have to make but a step between the pier and the steamboats. A dock of 3 acres, bounded by another pier, also provided with double lines of rails, is in a forward state, for the exclusive accommodation of merchandise and cattle. The Directors and their friends, after examining the station, proceeded to the Yarborough Arms for breakfast. This inn and a small ferry-house were until lately the only buildings to be seen at New Holland, where, for miles around, the country stretches out in all the flat luxuriance of a Flemish landscape. At 10.00 am the party took their places in a train of five carriages, for Grimsby, a distance of 16 miles. In the distance there are five intermediate stations. About 6 miles from New Holland we reached a spot where a junction will be formed with the line from Gainsborough and Sheffield, through Glanford Brigg. Passing into the Brocklesby domains, which the line intersects for nearly 8 miles, we came to Ulceby, where the New Holland Branch, on which we had been travelling, joins the main line by forming one side of a triangle. From New Holland, until we reached Grimsby, the route lies through country presenting no remarkable engineering difficulties, no heavy embankments or deep cuttings, the chief works being bridges and culverts for the accommodation of the many drains intersected. We arrived at Grimsby at about 10.45 am and were met on the platform by the Mayor and corporation of that ancient borough, and a party of Directors of the East Lincolnshire. The Grimsby Station is intended to be used jointly by the two companies, and is so situated that it may easily be extended at either extremity. After some delay, at about 2.00 pm

we proceeded to Louth, on the line of the East Lincolnshire. The distance from
Grimsby to Louth is 14 miles of nearly the most direct and level line in England.
The substantial but economical manner in which it has been executed reflects the
greatest credit on the Engineer. After a short stay at Louth we returned through
Grimsby to the dinner.

It must be observed that the East Lincolnshire line has been leased to the Great
Northern. So far these two railways only afford local accommodation for the traffic
passing between Hull, New Holland, Grimsby and the town of Louth; but in the
autumn it is expected that the GNR will have opened a complete communication
from Louth through Boston to Peterborough. When this communication is opened,
passengers, by the aid of the London and North Western and the Eastern Counties,
will be able to travel direct from Hull to the Metropolis, saving nearly 40 miles in
distance and about 10 shillings in money; while the Colonial produce for the use of
Lincolnshire may be transported from the London Docks direct, without transfer
until it reaches the last station of the Lincolnshire lines.

The *Stamford Mercury*, reported a corresponding journey taking place on
the same day in the opposite direction.

On Tuesday and Wednesday, 29th and 1st inst., the branch of the East Lincolnshire Railway, (extending 29 miles from Louth to New Holland, on the River
Humber) was opened to the public. The 1st March was the day appointed for the
commencement of trafic, but the day previously had been wisely appointed to the
pleasurable part of the business connected with the opening. John Deniston Esq.,
the indefatigable Secretary of the East Lincolnshire company, having politely
issued a considerable number of tickets to the principal inhabitants of Louth,
including the gentlemen constituting the Town Council, there were eight large first
and second class carriages and a luggage van, all of the most beautiful build to
which was prefixed a powerful engine, placed alongside of the temporary platform
erected near the gatehouse for the convenience of departure. 9.45 am was the time
announced when the train would precisely start, but the non-arrival of the southern part until half an hour afterwards caused a delay. At a quarter past 10 o'clock,
the signal was given and the whole cavalcade began to move as on a bowling green,
and increasing velocity, the train flew along the line at a rate varying between 20
and 30, and at one part 50 miles per hour so that, with the exception of trifling
stoppages allowing the Directors time to inspect the various beautiful village
stations along the line, passing objects and persons rather dazzled than afforded an
opportunity for even the most alert of the passengers to salute them. In about half
an hour the whole arrived at Grimsby station and were put in contrast, (much to
the advantage of the Louth train) with one from New Holland, which was soon on
its way to Louth. Half an hour after this (writes our correspondent) we moved on,
and, passing beneath the newly constructed bridge near Grimsby's church, our
vehicle passed Brocklesby park and mansion, the seat of Lord Yarborough. On
approaching our destination a slight accident gave the passengers an opportunity
of witnessing the dexterity of the train servants owing to some points not being so
nicely adjusted as was required, two of the carriages got off the rails, the passengers had to get out, and with the assistance of a short thick plank and the
movement of the engine coinciding, in a few minutes the carriages were helped on
the line and the train again connected. As soon as we arrived at New Holland,
where our appetites were sufficiently whetted by a fresh breeze, which had
continuously blown, the company sought a repast, but to many in vain, the host at
the inn not being able to supply the demand, and the visitors (including as I have
stated, several of the Town Council), luckily falling in with an old jack tar with
gingerbread buns on his stall, it was completely eaten up, with peculiar relish.

After viewing the port of Hull, which, with as pleasant an aspect invited the passengers over but which the duration of their stay forbade, so too an inspection of the extended jetty, which seemed as if it would stretch across the whole Humber. The whistle of the engine, equally out of tune with the temper of the passengers gave its significant notice and we were once again seated and in a trice we brought up in our return at Grimsby station. Here the passengers would have visited their friends but the usual uncertainty as to the time of departure prevented the indulgence. After waiting half an hour for the return from Louth of the New Holland train, it arrived and contained the Manchester, Sheffield and Lincolnshire Directors who retired with those of the East Lincolnshire to the Granby Inn, to settle some matters connected with the interests of the respective lines. This business occupied another half an hour during which interval Mr William Armitage,* of Louth, explained his explosive lights designed to give notice of dangers by night on the railway, to several scientific gentlemen. At length the time arrived for our ultimate return, we arrived at Louth, where were waiting for the company, two new omnibuses of Messrs Willoughby and Michael, we entered the handsome little bus belonging to the latter, (and built by Mr Markham, of Louth) and in a few minutes found ourselves at the Masons Arms Hotel, where was provided a dinner for the gentry connected with the line and their friends. The day following being market day at Louth, the fruits of the railway were strikingly apparent in the vast number of new faces seen in the market, numerous persons having availed themselves of the extraordinary facilities afforded by the railway travelling to visit Louth.

During 1849/50, the 1848 agreement between the GNR and the MS&LR, allowing each company's trains to run over the other's tracks, became the victim of more important national wrangling between the MS&LR, the GNR and the London and North Western, which saw the imminent opening of the Great Northern's London terminus as a great source of antagonism. The MS&LR did an about-face and aligned itself with the 'Euston Square Confederacy', (the London North Western, the Midland and the Lancashire and Yorkshire), in their campaign to block the GNR. The outcome of this was that the GNR's former ally now set itself upon a course of obstruction. The station authorities at Retford refused to supply water to GNR engines, so hampering the through service between Peterborough and Leeds. At Grimsby blocks were placed on the rails to prevent Great Northern trains entering the station, thus preventing through running to New Holland.

On at least one occasion when GNR passengers did reach New Holland, they found that the last ferry had been despatched without them, and they were forced to spend the night in the carriages or in the station. A High Court injunction against the MS&LR supported the GNR's rights to run to New Holland but did nothing to halt the obstructionist tactics. Through running by the MS&LR to Louth ceased on 8th July, 1851 and the GNR traffic between Grimsby and New Holland finished by 1st December of that year.

*See Chapter 14.

The Great Northern and the East Lincolnshire Railways.---Times of Dep

STATIONS.	DOWN TRAINS.								SUNDAY TRAINS.			FARES,	Market and Day Ti
	1 1, 2, 3 Par. Tr.	2* 1, 2, 3 Par. Tr.	3 1, 2	4† 1, 2	5 1, 2 Expres	6‡ 1, 2	7 1, 2	8 1, 2 Mail.	1 1, 2, 3. Par. Tr	2† 1. 2	3 1, 2. Mail	On Great Northern and East Lincolnshire Lines.	First and second cl. tickets are issued to Bos Lincoln from all the on the Great Norther
	A. M.	A. M.	A. M.	A. M.	A. M.	A. M.	P. M.	P. M.	A. M.	A. M.	P M.	Intermediate Fares for	and from the stations
LONDON, by Eastn. Counties,) Bishopgate-street, departure)				6 0		11 30	2 30	8 40	7 0	5 40		distances exceeding 6 miles by	East Lincolnshire Line b
LONDON, by L. & N. Western,) Euston-square ...... departure)				7 15	10 30	P. M.	4 0	9 0	7 30	9 0	Ordinary Trains —	Alford and Boston :—th ers of which are enti
CAMBRIDGE				9 34		1 48	5 25	10 40	9 50	10.49		1st Class 2d per mile.	travel by either ordin
ST. IVES				10 14		2 24						2nd Class 1½d.	express trains.
HUNTINGDON				10 35		2 40						Plus fractional parts of	Third Class Market
						A. M.						& 3d, and Government duty	Tickets.
NORWICH				7 40		11 0				6 30			are issued by the Parl
						P. M.							ary morning trains fr
ELY				10 20		2 25	6 40	11 31		10 35	11 31		stations on the Great N
BIRMINGHAM				8 0	10 30		2 30					FARES FROM LONDON.	Line every Wednesda
COVENTRY				8 30	11 10		3 15			11 37			Saturday to Lincoln, wb
						P. M.						1st. 2nd. 1st. 2nd. 3rd.	Friday to Lincoln, wh
NORTHAMPTON			7 0	10 25	1 3		6 30	11 40		10 35	11 40		title the holders to retu
				P. M.						A. M.		s. D. s. D. s. D. s. D. s. D.	by any Train after no
PETERBOROUGH -{ arrival { departure		6 20	9 0 9 10	12 15 12 30	2 45	3 55 4 15	8 30 8 40	1 15 1 36	8 0	4 0	1 15 1 30	16 6 13 0 7 6	being an express train. Hull. Trains leave for Man
WALTON, STAMFORD, and) LEICESTER junction ......)													Shetfield, York, Leeds
PEAKIRK and DEEPING		6 34	9 24	12 44		4 29	8 54		8 14	4 14		18 6 14 6	borough, or Bridlington, a
Littleworth and Deeping Fen ...		6 49	9 39	12 59		4 44	9 9		8 20	4 29		20 2 15 6	a.m., 12.45, 1.50. and
SPALDING		7 0	9 50	1 10	3 20	4 55	9 20	2 16	8 40	4 40	2 16	21 6 17 0 20 1 16 0	p.m.; and arrive at
SUTTERTON, ALGARKIRK,) SWINESHD.&DONNINGS)		7 20	10 5	1 25	3 35	5 15	9 40		9 0	5 0		23 6 18 0 21 9 16 11	7.10, and 9. 50 a.m., 2.45, and 5.45 p.m.
BOSTON ....arrival		7 35	10 20	1 40	3 50	5 30	9 55	2 51	9 15	5 15	2 51	25 0 19 6 23 4 17 8	Lincoln.
BOSTON ... dep. for LINCOLN		7 45	10 25	1 50	4 0	5 40	10 0		9 25	5 20			Trains leave for Newar
Langrick		8 0	10 40	2 5		5 55			9 40	5 35		23 10 18 6	tingham, and Derby at
Dogdyke		8 15	10 55			6 10			9 55	5 50			5.15; and 8.30 (Mail),
TATTERSHALL		8 20	10 58	2 23	4 20	6 13	10 20		9 58	5 53		26 6 20 4 24 1 18 9	and arrive at Lincoln at
KIRKSTEAD & HORNCASTLE		8 29	11 6	2 31	4 30	6 21	10 30		10 6	6 1		26 6 20 4 25 5 19 3	a.m. 1.45, 5.20. and 7.
Stixwould		8 35	11 11	2 36		6 26			10 11	6 6		25 5 19 3	Day Tickets.
Southry		8 41	11 16	2 41		6 31			10 16	6 11		25 5 19 10	Available only. by this
BARDNEY, for WRAGBY		8 48	11 22	2 47		6 37			10 22	6 17		25 11 19 10	trains, are issued, at 2
Five-mile House..............		8 50	11 31	2 56		6 46			10 31	6 26		26 6 20 4	on Tuesdays and Friday
Washingborough...............		9 6	11 38	3		6 53			10 38	6 33		26 0 20 4	Grimsby to Hull and for
LINCOLN .... arrival		9 15	11 45	10	6	7 0	11 0	P. M.	10 45	6.40		26 0 20 4 26 6 20 4 12 7	vice versa. Upon the
LINCOLN ....depart. for HULL			9 0	12		4 25		9 5	8 0				journey, the Passenge
Washingborough..............			9 5			4 30		9 11	8 5				shew the Ticket in the
Five-mile House...............			9 11					9 18	8 11				office to have it re-stan
Bardney, for Wragby			9 21					9 29	8 21				the clerk, before he
Southry			9 26			4 51		9 35	8 26				the carriage, without w
Stixwould			9 31			4 56		9 41	8 31				will not be allowed as
KIRKSTEAD & HORNCASTLE			9 36	12 27		5 1		9 47	8 36				ticket. Nor will he
TATTERSHALL			9 44	12 35		5 8		9 55	8 44				lowed to stop at inter
Dogdyke			9 47			5 11			8 47				stations, and go forward
Langrick			10 2			5 20			8 51				ther train.
BOSTON .... arrival			10 15	1 0		5 35		10 20	9 15				Luggage.
BOSTON ... departure for HULL		7 45	10 20	1 45	4 0	5 40		2 51	9 25	5 20	2 51		The companies do no themselves responsible
Sibsey...................		7 55	10 30	1 55		5 50			9 40	5 35		24 4 18 6	gage, unless booked a
Old Leake and Wrangle		8 0	10 35	2 0		5 55			9 44	5 39		24 11 19 0	for according to its
East Ville and New Leake		8 8	10 43	2 8		6 3			9 53	5 48		25 5 19 0	Each 1st and 2nd class
Little Steeping.................		8 16	10 51	2 16		6 11			10 1	5 56		25 11 19 6	ger is allowed 100 lb
FIRSBY, SPILSBY, WAINFLEET		8 22	10 57	2 22	4 26	6 17		3 34	10 8	6 3	3 34	28 6 22 6 26 6 19 10	each Parliamentary cl
BURGH........................		8 27	11 2	2 27	4 30	6 22		3 38	10 13	6 9	3 38	28 6 22 6 26 6 20 0	senger 56 lbs. weight
Willoughby.....................		8 34	11 9	2 34		6 29			10 22	6 17		27 0 20 6	gage free of charge, no
ALFORD		8 43	11 18	2 43	4 41	6 38		3 53	10 30	6 25	3 53	30 0 23 6 27 0 20 10	merchandise or other
Claythorpe.....................		8 50	11 25	2 50		6 45			10 39	6 34		28 0 21 5	carried for hire or pro
Authorpe		8 56	11 31	2 56		6 51			10 45	6 40		28 0 21 5	excess above the wei
Lezbourne		9 2	11 36	3 1		6 56			10 53	6 48		29 0 21 11	be charged at ¼d per lb
LOUTH	7 15	9* 9	11 44	3 9	5 1	7 6		4 26	11 6	6 56	4 26	32 6 25 3 29 6 22 2 13 0	and Peterborough; an
Ludborough	7 26	9 20	11 54	3 20		7 16			11 17	7 7		30 6 23 0	lb.to stations on other r
NORTH THORESBY	7 32	9 26	11 59	3 26	5 16	7 21			11 22	7 12		34 0 26 6 30 8 23 3	Passengers are strongly
Holton-le-Clay and Tetney......	7 38	9 32	12 3	3 33		7 28			11 28	7 18		31 2 23 6	mended to have their
Waltham and Humberstone	7 43	9 38	12 10	3 38		7 33			11 27	7 22		31 2 23 9	and destinations clearly
GREAT GRIMSBY	7 49	9 45	12 15	3 45	5 32	7 40		4 59	11 34	7 29	4 59	35 0 27 0 31 6 24 0 14 0	upon their luggage, and
Great Cotes....................	7 55	9 51	12 21	3 51		7 45			11 39	7 34		32 0 24 4 14 0	tice the number of the
Stallingborough	8 1	9 57	12 27	3 57		7 50			11 44	7 39		32 3 24 4 14 0	carriage in or upon wh
Habrough	8 10	10 6	12 36	4 6		7 56			11 51	7 46		32 11 25 0 14 0	placed.
ULCEBY, MARKET RASEN jetn.	8 15	10 12	12 42	4 12	5 50	8 1		5 21	11 56	7 51	5 21	33 0 25 0 33 2 25 3 14 0	Parcels
Goxhill	8 24	10 21	12 51	4 21		8 10			12 5			33 11 25 9 14 0	Must be delivered at
New Holland	8 30	10 30	1 0	4 30	6 7	8 15		5 36	12 4	8 5	5 36	34 2 25 9 14 0	spective stations ten
HULL ....arrival about	9 0	11 0	1 30	5 0	6 37	8 45		6 6	12 40	8 35	6 6	35 0 27 0 34 4 26 0 14 0	before the departure trains by which they ar forwarded.

* 1 & 2 Class between Louth and Hull.   † Parl'y Train from London, to Lincoln, to Louth, and stations between Great Grimsby and Hull only.   ‡ Parliamentary Train between Grimsby and Hull.

The Great Northern and East Lincolnshire Railways' timetable for 1st March, 1849.

Arrival from the 1st of March, 1849, until further notice.

	UP TRAINS.									SUNDAY TRAINS.			FARES FROM HULL.				
Passengers, intsure being booked, should	STATIONS.	**1** 1, 2, 3 Par. Tr.	**2+** 1, 2, 3 Par. Tr.	**3*** 1, 2 Mail.	**4** 1, 2 Exprs	**5*** 1, 2	**6** 1, 2	**7*** 1, 2 Mail.	**1** 1, 2, 3 Par. Tr.	**2'** 1, 2	**3** 1, 2 Mail.	EXPRESS. 1st. 2nd.		ORDINARY. 1st. 2nd. 3rd.			

[Left margin column of regulations text:]

Passengers, insure being booked, should t the stations five minutes er than the advertised times parturo.

doors of the booking offices be closed punctually at the fixed for the departure of rain, after which no person be admitted.

Carriages and Horses eyed to and from all first stations.

Passengers ig in their own Carriages rst-class fare.

Grooms g the care of horses will harged according to the age they ride in, but when lling in the same box with horses, they will be ed third-class fares.

Carriages and Horses ages and horses must be e station fifteen minutes e the time of starting of rains.

riage Trucks and horse Boxes usually kept at all the car stations; but to prevent pointment, it is requisite otice should be given the previous at the station they will be required.

Smoking rictly prohibited at the os or in the carriages, a penalty of 40s.

ssenger will be allowed to a carriage after the train motion.

atuity, under any circumstances, is permitted to be by any servant of the any.

ngers and parcels booked 45, Queen-street, Hull, various stations on the where every information e obtained.

Goods. ll parts of Lincolnshire, or London, Cambridge, Huntingdon, Norwich, ampton, Coventry, Birmingham, &c., are received at ondon and North Western the Eastern Counties ns and Offices, in London sewhere; at the Manchester, Sheffield, and Lincolnshire Company's Warehouse, klin Creek, Hull; and at spective stations; where and information may be as also at 45, Queen-Hull, the passenger sta-

dren under 3 years of conveyed Free, and those 3 and under 12 conveyed fare.

List of Coaches, Omnibuses, next page.

[Main timetable — UP Trains:]

STATIONS	1	2+	3*	4	5*	6	7*	1	2'	3	1st	2nd	1st	2nd	3rd
	A.M.	A.M.	A.M.	A.M.	P.M.	P.M.	P.M.	A.M.	P.M.	P.M.	s. d.	s. d.	s. d.	s. d.	s. d.
HULL..........departure	...	6 40	8 15	10 30	1 0	3 30	7 0	8 15	4 0	7 0	...	...	...	...	...
New Holland	...	7 10	8 45	11 0	1 30	4 0	7 30	8 45	4 30	7 30	...	...	0 6 0 4	0 4	
Goxhill	...	7 15	8 50	...	1 35	4 5	7 35	8 50	4 35	7 35	...	...	1 0 0 8	0 6½	
ULCEBY, MARKET RASEN jctn.	...	7 26	9 1	11 14	1 46	4 16	7 46	9 1	4 46	7 46	2 2 1 8	1 6 1 1	0 10½		
Habreugh	...	7 81	9 7	...	1 52	4 22	7 52	9 7	4 52	7 52	...	...	1 10 1 4	1 0	
Stallingborough	...	7 40	9 17	...	2 0	4 31	8 1	9 17	5 1	8 1	...	...	2 4 1 8	1 3	
Great Cotes	...	7 46	9 23	...	2 6	4 37	8 6	9 23	5 7	8 6	...	...	2 9 1 10	1 5	
GREAT GRIMSBY	...	7 52	9 29	11 32	2 10	4 42	8 12	9 29	5 12	8 12	3 6 3 0	3 0 2 1	1 7		
Waltham and Humberstone	...	7 59	9 36	...	...	4 49	8 19	9 36	5 19	8 19	...	...	3 9 2 7	1 10	
Holton-le-Clay, and Tetney	...	8 4	9 42	...	2 20	4 55	8 24	9 42	5 25	8 24	...	...	4 0 2 10	2 0	
NORTH THORESBY	...	8 9	9 48	11 46	2 25	5 0	8 29	9 48	5 30	8 29	5 6 4 6	4 6 3 1	2 2		
Ludborough	...	8 14	9 54	...	...	5 4	8 34	9 54	5 34	8 34	...	...	4 6 3 3	2 3½	
LOUTH	...	8 27	10 10	12 2	2 38	5 18	8 48	10 10	5 48	8 48	6 6 5 6	5 6 3 10	2 9		
Legbourne	...	8 33	10 16	...	...	5 24	...	10 16	5 54	...	...	...	6 0 4 4	2 11½	
Authorpe	...	8 43	10 25	...	2 50	5 33	...	10 25	6 3	...	...	...	6 8 4 7	3 3	
Claythorpe	...	8 48	10 29	...	...	5 37	...	10 29	6 7	...	...	...	7 2 4 10	3 4	
ALFORD	...	9 3	10 38	12 23	3 0	5 46	9 22	10 39	6 16	9 22	9 0 7 3	7 3 5 3	3 7		
Willoughby	...	9 11	10 46	...	3 10	5 54	...	10 47	6 24	...	...	...	7 8 5 9	3 10	
BURGH	...	9 21	10 55	12 34	3 20	6 3	9 42	10 56	6 33	9 42	10 0 8 6	8 9 6 3	4 1		
FIRSBY, SPILSBY, WAINFLEET	...	9 29	11 0	12 39	3 28	6 8	9 48	11 2	6 38	9 48	10 6 8 6	8 9 6 4	4 3½		
Little Steeping	...	9 36	11 6	...	3 33	6 14	...	11 8	6 44	...	...	...	9 3 6 9	4 5½	
East Villa and New Leake	...	9 40	11 15	...	3 42	6 23	...	11 18	6 53	...	...	...	9 10 7 0	4 9	
Old Leake and Wrangle	...	9 55	11 24	...	3 50	6 32	...	11 27	7 2	...	...	...	10 4 7 5	5 0	
Sibsey	...	10 0	11 29	...	3 55	6 37	10 19	11 33	7 7	10 19	...	...	10 10 7 10	5 1½	
BOSTON..........arrival	...	10 15	11 44	1 1	4 10	6 52	10 34	11 48	7 22	10 34	13 6 11 0	11 5 8 4	5 7		
BOSTON... dep. for LINCOLN	...	10 25	...	1 50	5 40	...	10 0	5 20 P.M.	...	...					
Langrick	...	10 40	...	2 5	5 55	...	...	5 35	...	...					
Dogdyke	...	10 55	...	6 10	...	...	...	5 50	...	...					
TATTERSHALL	...	10 58	...	2 23	6 13	...	10 20	5 53	...	...					
KIRKSTEAD & HORNCASTLE	...	11 6	...	2 31	6 21	...	10 30	6 1	...	...	*On Great Northern and East*				
Stixwould	...	11 11	...	2 36	6 26	...	...	6 6	...	...	*Lincolnshire Lines.*				
Southry	...	11 16	...	2 41	6 31	...	...	6 11	...	...					
Bardney, for Wragby	...	11 22	...	2 47	6 37	...	...	6 17	...	...	**.* Intermediate Fares for*				
Five-mile House	...	11 31	...	2 56	6 46	...	...	6 26	...	...	distances exceeding 6 miles by				
Washingborough	...	11 38	...	3 3	6 53	...	...	6 33	...	...	Ordinary Trains:—				
LINCOLN..........arrival	...	11 45	...	3 10	7 0	...	11 0	6 40	...	...	1st Class......2d. per mile.				
LINCOLN...dep. for LONDON	7 30	9 0	...	12 0	3 0	4 25	9 5	8 0	5 55		2nd Class......1½d. "				
Washingborough	7 36	9 5	...	...	3 5	4 30	9 11	8 5	6 1		Plus fractional parts of 6d. and				
Five-mile House	7 43	9 11	...	...	3 11	4 36	9 18	8 11	6 8		3d. and Government Duty.				
BARDNEY, for WRAGBY	7 54	9 21	...	...	3 21	4 46	9 29	8 21	6 19						
Southry	8 0	9 26	...	...	3 26	4 51	9 35	8 26	6 25						
Stixwould	8 6	9 31	...	...	3 31	4 56	9 41	8 31	6 31						
KIRKSTEAD & HORNCASTLE	8 11	9 36	...	12 27	3 36	5 1	9 47	8 36	6 36						
TATTERSHALL	8 20	9 44	...	12 35	3 41	5 8	9 55	8 44	6 45						
Dogdyke	8 23	9 47	...	...	3 44	5 11	...	8 47	6 48						
Langrick	8 36	10 2	...	...	4 0	5 20	...	9 2	7 1						
BOSTON..........arrival	8 50	10 15	...	1 0	4 15	5 35	10 20	9 15	7 15						
								A.M.	P.M.						
BOSTON. dep. for PETERBORO'	9 5	10 25	11 50	1 10	4 20	7 0	10 35	11 55	7 30	10 35	...	...	...		
SUTTERTON, ALGARKIRK, SWINESHEAD, and DONNINGTON	9 20	10 40	12 5	1 25	4 35	7 15	10 54	12 10	7 46	10 54	15 6 12 3	13 0 9 5	6 1½		
SPALDING	9 35	10 56	12 20	1 40	4 50	7 30	11 15	12 30	8 4	11 15	17 0 13 6	14 0 10 1	6 9		
Littleworth and Deeping Fen	9 50	11 10	12 32	...	5 0	7 40	11 27	12 42	8 16	11 27	...	...	15 0 11 2	7 5	
PEAKIRK and DEEPING	10 5	11 24	12 45	...	5 15	7 55	11 40	12 56	8 33	11 40	...	...	16 2 9	7 8	
WALTON, STAMFORD, and LEICESTER junction	...	...	...	...	...	...	...	...	...	...					
PETERBOROUGH arrival / departure	10 20 10 30	11 40 11 55	1 0	2 15 2 30	5 25 5 30	8 10	11 55 ...	1 10 12 5	3 50	11 55 12 5	22 0 17 6	18 2 13 1	8 2½		
NORTHAMPTON	...	...	...	...	7 15	...	...	1 48	...	...	1 48	29 3 23 0	25 5 18 7	...	
COVENTRY	2 50	...	...	...	...	...	...	...	...	...	31 3 24 3	27 5 19 10	...		
BIRMINGHAM	3 45	...	...	...	...	...	...	...	...	...	33 6 25 9	29 8 22 1	...		
ELY	...	...	1 13	...	4 10	6 55	...	1 25	5 24	...	1 25	28 3 22 6	24 5 18 1	...	
NORWICH	...	...	4 50	...	8 35	10 40	...	...	8 35	...	...	39 6 31 3	35 8 27 1	...	
HUNTINGDON	...	...	1 0	...	...	6 50	...	...	...	...	...	30 0 23 6	26 0 19 0	...	
St. IVES	...	...	1 20	...	...	7 3	...	...	...	...	...	30 6 24 6	26 6 18 10	...	
CAMBRIDGE	...	...	1 58	...	4 10	7 42	...	1 50	6 5	...	1 50	31 3 25 0	27 5 20 7	...	
LONDON, by Eastn. Counties, arrival / LONDON, by L. & N. Western arrival / Euston-square, arrival	8 0	...	4 20	...	6 25	11 0	...	4 26 ... 4 45	9 40 9 50	...	4 26 4 45	35 0 27 0 34 6 26 0 14 0 / 45 0 27 0 34 6 26 0 14 0			

The original bridge over the River Witham, at Boston, from the engraving by R. E. Creasey, c.1850.   *Alan Turner*

An engraving of Boston dated October 1848.   *Author's Collection*

104.—EAST LINCOLNSHIRE.

Incorporated by 10 Vic., cap. 88 (26th July, 1846). Commences (in conjunction with the Great Northern loop) at Boston, and terminates (in conjunction with the Manchester Sheffield and Lincolnshire) at Great Grimsby—18 miles; opened from Grimsby to Louth, 14 miles, 1st March; from Louth to Firsby, 12 miles, 3rd September; and the remainder from Firsby to Boston Junction, 15 miles, 1st October, 1848.

This company by 10 and 11 Vic., cap. 113, and under sanction of the lessees, who are the responsible parties, purchased the unexpired interest of Messrs. F. and G. Chaplin, in the lease held by them for 48 years, commencing from 28th August, 1828, in the Louth Navigation; also of the unexpired lease of a piece of land, known as "Mallard Ings," held by Mr. Thomas Chaplin for 99 years, commencing from 9th April, 1800, the consideration paid being an annuity of 1,500l. for the unexpired term and an assumption of the bond debt of the canal, supposed to be 1,500l. per annum.

By 11 Vic., cap. 125, power was given to make the Great Grimsby branch and Sheffield Junction half a mile additional length.

Under 11 Vic., cap. 148 (1847), this line has been leased in perpetuity to the Great Northern at a fixed rental of 36,000l. per annum, equal to 6 per cent. per annum on the share capital (fixed capital of 600,000l.) from 1st October, 1848; the G.N. providing all extra cost of construction, and assuming the loan debt. Lease is dated February 21st, 1848, and the terms are repeated in sec. 34 of 13 Vic., cap. 84, which gives this company right to repossess, on non-payment of the rent for seven months, from 1st April and 1st October. Meantime the G.N. pay all expenses connected with the registration of transfers, the distribution of dividend, and all other administrative charges attending the same.

Extract from the 1871 *Bradshaw's Shareholders Manual.*

Chapter Four
The Development of Boston

The River Witham, and the use of the river (from Lincoln and beyond) for wool and other exports, made Boston a mediaeval boom town. At the time of the Domesday Book it did not exist but by 1205, according to the evidence of a tax raised on the goods of merchants, it was second only to London as a port of importance. Its great annual fair was an attraction for traders from all over England and the Continent.

Things had taken a dramatic turn by 1571 when the corporation was claiming that Boston was so destitute of ships and trade that it was likely to fall into utter ruin. This theme was continued in 1607 when Parliament was petitioned asking for the town's name to be put on the list of decayed towns. However, things were not quite as bad as the picture painted by the corporation, there was a steady import trade in spices, Brazilian wood, French and Spanish wines and Norwegian deal. Exports consisted of hempseed and linseed, glue, uncast lead, leather, sheepskins and butter. The 18th and 19th centuries saw improvements to the inland waterways and to the outfall through the Wash and a thriving trade in corn, coal and other goods. Its importance as a local market and administrative centre, together with the establishment of manufacturing industries in the early 19th century, saw the population rise from about 3,000 in the early 18th century to 15,000 by 1851.

Whereas at Grimsby the MS&LR invested in the creation of the docks, at Boston development was undertaken by the local community. John Calbourn Simonds and his son William achieved dominant positions in the corporation and set out to provide a dock for the town. In 1879 the corporation reached agreement with the drainage commissioners to improve the haven between Boston and the Wash. The following year an Act was obtained for a dock at the southern end of Boston. In June 1882 Mrs Simonds cut the first sod on the site of Boston dock and the first ship entered the seven acre basin on 15th December, 1884. The GNR did not participate in the scheme; even though Boston was the company's chief revenue earning station in the county, not until 1903 did they increase the size of their goods shed and provide extra sidings.

The number of vessels entering the port rose from 396, in 1881, to 605 in 1894. The chief imports were grain, fruit, timber and oilseed whilst oilcake, potatoes, iron and coal were the chief exports. Much of the timber came from the Baltic in the form of sleepers and was treated at the GNR's sleeper depot which had moved to a new, larger, site at Hall Hills, just north of Boston, in 1900.

Small fishing smacks had operated from Boston since the early 19th century and from the 1880s steam trawlers and drifters appeared. The Boston Deep Sea Fishing and Ice Company, started by local businessmen in 1885, came to dominate the industry at the port; it built an ice factory, various workshops and offices and the fish pontoon and employed over 500 men.

Boston was the early centre of much of the GNR's activity in Lincolnshire, the Corporation records first refer to the railways in 1844, although as early as 1836 a scheme to bring Boston into railway contact with Nottingham and London was introduced, but came to nothing. In 1844 a proposal was made to link Wakefield, Lincoln and Boston and in 1845/46 came another for a London and York loop line, to run from Peterborough northwards through Spalding, Boston and Lincoln, to Bawtry, near Doncaster. Also in 1846 the Ambergate, Nottingham and Boston and Eastern Junction Railway was promoted to run from Ambergate, near Belper, in Derbyshire, to Spalding, via Nottingham and Grantham, with branches to Boston and Sleaford. In the same year plans were drawn up for the East Lincolnshire Railway and the Eastern Counties, Cambridge to Lincoln line, running via Spalding and Heckington, with a branch to Boston.

The 1844 Wakefield, Lincoln and Boston proposals were adopted by the London and York promoters (later the GNR), at a meeting in Normanton in August 1844. Although the scheme was rejected by Parliament in 1845, by 1846 it had gained widespread support in Boston, at the expense of the Cambridge and Lincoln scheme. In the 1846 session of Parliament both the GNR and the East Lincolnshire Bills were passed on 26th June.

The first sections of line close to Boston were laid on the Lincolnshire loop between Boston and Lincoln. Work began at various points along the line in the spring of 1847, it being envisaged that the complete line between Peterborough and Gainsborough would be open by the end of February 1848. During the first week in February 1847, vessels began arriving at Boston laden with pig iron and timber for the GNR. The pig iron was taken by barge along the River Witham, to the GNR foundry at Lincoln to be made into chairs. The timber was cut into sleepers at workshops beside the Grand Sluice, at Boston. Railway materials continued to arrive in great quantities, some being unloaded at Boston, the rest going through the Grand Sluice to various parts of the line.

Construction work at the Boston end of the ELR began in October 1847, when piles were driven into the bed of the River Witham in preparation for the railway bridge. The arrival of several thousand navvies around Boston so alarmed the magistrates that they warned householders to take great care by locking their houses at night!

The following month, 400 labourers were discharged because they were unwilling to continue to work, 'in the present alarming state of affairs in the monetary world'. Companies all over the country were taking similar action, in the slump following the 'railway mania' of the previous year.

Work was progressing well on the loop line to the north of Boston, however, although the railway had to cross the river and the Grand Sluice Bridge was not yet complete. This work was completed by February 1848, and on 10th March the first train consisting of 72 ballast wagons crossed the Grand Sluice. A few days later the GNR had eight Baltic vessels discharging wood for sleepers; it was said that the oldest sailor in Boston could not remember seeing so many large vessels in the port on one spring tide.

Even at this stage no decision had been taken regarding the siting of the station. It was feared that the high prices demanded for land might force the

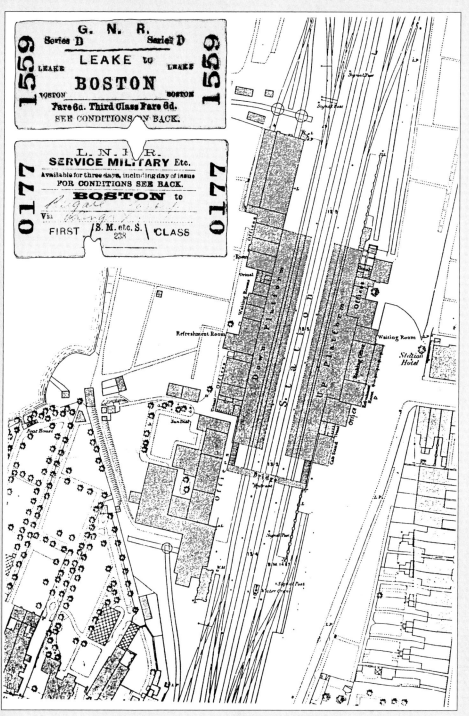

The 1887 map of Boston station.   *Courtesy 1887, 25" Ordnance Survey map*

A 1906 survey of Boston station giving a good comparison of facilities, to the map on the previous page. *Courtesy 1906, 25" Ordnance Survey map*

GNR class 'F2' 0−4−2 mixed traffic engine No. 50, allocated to Boston in 1905 and seen here at work; the wagons are marked 'Turner, Boston'.
P. W. Pilcher Collection, National Railway Museum

GNR Ivatt single No. 265, the last class of single wheelers to be built in Britain, on an express working at Boston.   *P. W. Pilcher Collection, National Railway Museum*

ROBERTS'S GREAT NORTHERN

AND EAST LINCOLNSHIRE

RAILWAY ADVERTISER.

No. 1.]   MARCH 1, 1849.   [PRICE ONE PENNY.

LEWIN'S Compound Fluid Extract of
SARSAPARILLA,
CAREFULLY PREPARED BY STEAM.

THIS convenient and elegant preparation of Sarsaparilla is prescribed and recommended by the most eminent Physicians in Cutaneous Eruptions, in cases of debility, and as an excellent Tonic and Restorative after the use of Mercury. One table-spoonful of this Extract contains the strength of half a pint of the Compound Decoction as usually prepared.

Sold in Bottles at 2s. 6d. and 5s. each, by
E.C.Lewin, Chemist, Market-place, Boston.

C. & T. WRIGHT,
HIGH-STREET, BOSTON,
Wholesale and Furnishing Ironmongers, Cut and Color Men, Dealers in Pig, Bar, Rod, Hoop, and Sheet Iron.
Stock kept of Eave Spouting and Piping. A quantity of bent Lancewood Shafts, always on hand.

Agents for Milner's Fire-Resisting Deed Boxes; Vergette's Water-proof Patent Wagon Covers; Gardner's Turnip Cutters; and Nicholson's Patent Wedge Cake Breakers.

Shower, Hip, and other Baths for Sale or Hire.

To the Nobility, Clergy, & Gentry, of the County of Lincoln.

EXTENSIVE SALE

OF

Cabinet and Upholstery

FURNITURE.

IN consequence of JOHN PEARSON being about to decline the above businesses, he is now offering the whole of his Stock of Cabinet and Upholstery Goods, which is one of the largest in the county, at greatly reduced prices, giving to the public an opportunity of rare occurrence, of selecting from so extensive a stock of really sound and good Furniture, in English Oak, Rosewood, Zebrawood, Mahogany, &c., the whole of which have been made of the best materials, and finished with the greatest care.

New Buildings, Market-place, Boston.
February 20, 1849.

Refreshment Rooms, Boston Station.

IT is respectfully announced to the Railway Travellers, via Great Northern, that Tea, Coffee, Soup, and other Refreshments, can be obtained at the Boston Station.

Passengers by the early Trains can obtain a comfortable breakfast at the usual charge.

Boston Station, Feb. 27, 1849.

NOTICE !!

W. GIBSON & SON, have lately made arrangements with the Eastern Counties Railway Company for daily conveyance of Goods, from London, Norfolk and all parts of Cambridgeshire to Sleaford, via Boston, at very low rates. W. G. & S. leave the White Horse Inn, Boston, every morning, 9 a.m., where further information may be obtained.

BOSTON! BOSTON!! BOSTON!!!

HAVE YOU BEEN TO

NO. 1.

SMALL'S

Hong Kong Tea Establishment,

MARKET-PLACE, BOSTON.

THE crowds and numbers who still continue to throng T. Small's Establishment, are powerful and striking proofs the goods are decidedly Cheap and of Sterling Quality. All persons studying the purchase of durable articles, combined with cheapness, are requested to call, when they will be shown goods that must amply repay for their trouble.

Business at this Establishment is conducted upon a three-fold grand and self-lasting principle—

Confidence! Quality! Cheapness!

T. Small has now on hand an extensive variety of well and carefully selected Teas—Picked Teas—Picked with judgment. All persons who enjoy and really desire Tea in its purity, strength, and freshness, should apply to T. S., who is thoroughly acquainted with every shade of taste, and prides himself on being able to suit all persons from the peasant to the prince.— The assertion is made—It is for you to make the trial. Be particular to say whether you use hard or soft water. It is now becoming a well known fact, that in order to have good articles at the lowest shade of profit, you have only to purchase at SMALL'S,

No. 1.
HONG KONG TEA ESTABLISHMENT,
MARKET-PLACE, BOSTON.
•.• OLD NEWSPAPERS BOUGHT.

Boston Railway Station, Great Northern.
W. MARTIN, News Agent, respectfully announces to his friends and the Railway Public that he has been appointed News Agent at the Boston Station, Great Northern Railway, where it will be his study to cater the cheapest and choicest literary food, for his patrons, the Railway Travellers.

W. M. has been appointed agent for ROBERTS's GREAT NORTHERN RAILWAY ADVERTISER AND TIME TABLE," which he will be able to supply on the first of every month, wholesale and retail.

GREAT NORTHERN & EAST LINCOLNSHIRE RAILWAY STATIONS.

THE SALT TRADE.

E. CLEMENT

BEGS respectfully to inform Buyers of this Article that he is now enabled to supply them with it, in a superior condition, for ready money. And retailers of Ale are respectfully informed that they can be supplied with a genuine article, at the lowest cash prices, at his
BREWERY, in ROSEGARTH-ST.
FAMILY ALE & BEER.
Wormgate, Boston, 1849.

CHEAP PROVISION WAREHOUSE,
WIDE BARGATE, BOSTON.

N. ALLEN,
Grocer, and Provision Dealer,

RETURNS his sincere thanks to his Friends and the Public generally, for the liberal encouragement he has received since his commencement, and assures them it shall be his constant endeavour to merit a continuance of their favors and to deserve their future support, by keeping the best goods only, and selling at such prices as will not fail to convince that a fair and honest system of doing business will bear all puffing and trickery.

A LARGE STOCK OF
PRIME CIGARS, TOBACCO, & FANCY SNUFFS.
CONFECTIONERY,
Wholesale and Retail.
GENUINE BRITISH WINES.
PICKLES AND FISH SAUCES,
In great variety.
FOREIGN FRUITS OF EVERY DESCRIPTION

Town and Country Shops and Hawkers supplied with the smallest quantities at Wholesale Prices.

Reproduction of the first issue of *Roberts' Great Northern and East Lincolnshire Railway Advertiser.* Robert Roberts was a printer and bookseller of Bargate in Boston.
Author's Collection

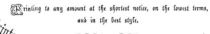
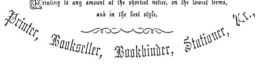

A GNR class 'E2' No. 213, on an express working at Boston. Based at Peterborough in 1905 and later at Boston, the engine was withdrawn from service in 1912.
P. W. Pilcher Collection, National Railway Museum

Stirling 8 foot single, 4−2−2, No. 1004; shedded at Peterborough throughout its life, No. 1004 was one of the last three surviving singles lasting until 1914. It is seen here at Boston shed in the early 1900s. *Alan Turner*

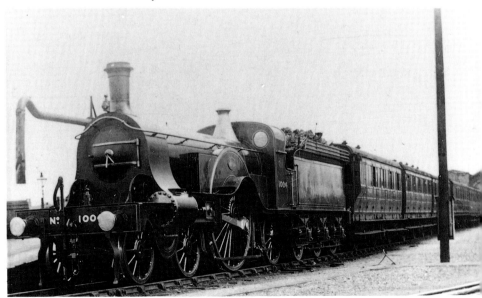

THE GREAT NORTHERN & EAST LINCOLNSHIRE RAILWAYS.

Superintendent's Office,

Lincoln, 19th Dec., 1849.

Special Order.

DISTANCE SIGNALS.

The Down Distance Signals are to be kept lighted at Spalding, Boston, Firsby, Alford, Louth, and Great Grimsby, until the Down Mail Train shall have passed.

The Up Distance Signals, are to be kept lighted at *the above Stations*, until the Up Mail, and Last Goods Train, shall have passed.

The Up and Down Signals, at all the other Stations, are to be kept lighted until the Up Mail Train, and the Last Passengers and Goods Trains, shall have passed.

Signalling Directive issued by The Great Northern and East Lincolnshire Railways, December 1849.

Left: Notice of Shareholders' Meeting, 1846.

EAST LINCOLNSHIRE RAILWAY.

NOTICE IS HEREBY GIVEN, that a General Meeting of the SHARE or SCRIP HOLDERS of this Company will be held at the Crown and Anchor Tavern, in the Strand, in the City of Westminster, on Saturday, the ninth day of May next, at One o'Clock precisely, for the purpose of receiving a copy of the Bill now before Parliament, for the Incorporation of this Company; and of taking the sense of the Proprietary upon the subject of proceeding further therewith.

The Directors desire to notify for the guidance of the Scripholders, that it is necessary that they should either attend in person and bring their Scrip, or send it to the Meeting by some other person, who, on producing Scrip, will be entitled to vote in respect thereof, and, as the Resolutions of the two Houses of Parliament require the Votes to be recorded with great minuteness, for the purpose of shewing the amount of Scrip held by each person present, whether in his own right or as another's representative, every bearer of Scrip attending, is requested to furnish the Secretary, before the commencement of the Meeting, with his Scrip, (in exchange for which a Receipt will be given), and with his name and address. The Scrip will be returned to the bearer of the Receipt on application at the Office of the Company, any day after the Meeting, between the hours of Eleven and Three.

By Order.

THOMAS REYNOLDS,

Secretary.

Dated 29th April, 1846,

Offices,—No. 4, Charing Cross, London.

Note.—To facilitate the arrangements at the Meeting, the Secretary will attend at the Offices of the Company every day previous to the Meeting, from 11 to 3 o'Clock, to receive and register the Scrip.

A GNR class 'E2' locomotive and short train crossing the Grand Sluice at Boston. Of particular interest are the elegant GNR somersault

GNR to build outside the borough in the Skirbeck Quarter; further cause for delay concerned problems crossing West Street. Although the GNR and the ELR had originally planned to have separate stations in Boston they eventually agreed to form a shared line and use the same station. The plan was for the shared line to cross West Street at the Bond Street junction. This scheme implied crossing the River Witham south of the Grand Sluice, rather than the original northern crossing, but this was thrown out by the Admiralty due to navigational problems, and both companies settled for crossing West Street west of the Queen Street junction.

By late June 1848, sufficient land had been bought just north of West Street level crossing to allow work to begin on a temporary station. The foundations were laid in August, and by late September 500 men were at work night and day to complete the station. The finished station had two 500 ft long platforms, as well as a water tank and large carriage shed. The Corporation Records stated, 'The establishment of the station of the GNR upon this street has added much to its stir and business like appearance'. Although the timing of completion of the work on the station was geared to the arrival of the GNR loop line, it was actually the ELR which first ran into the town. On 2nd October, 1848 many spectators saw the first train leave Boston at 7.35 am for Hull (via the New Holland ferry).

A great celebration was planned on 26th October, principally to mark the arrival of the GNR in Boston, however the ELR was well represented at the festivities and pleasure trips to Grimsby proved just as popular as those to Lincoln and Peterborough. There were the usual celebrations which accompanied the openings of railways, a public holiday, children parading through the streets being regaled with cakes and buns, and many celebratory dinners. The main public dinner was held at the theatre, among the distinguished guests being John Noble, the mayor of Boston, the Earl of Yarborough, Sir James Duke, R.A. Christopher, Edmund Denison, Charles Chaplin, W. Cubitt, G.H. Packe, R. Baxter and the Mayors of both Louth and Grimsby. Toasts were offered to just about everyone, but there were two speeches which offered a degree of contention, which no doubt livened up the proceedings somewhat. The Reverend Oldrid said that he hoped steps would be taken by the companies to do away with Sunday travelling and that the GNR and ELR would furnish Boston with a railway church and clergyman. He said it did his heart good to see what had been done at Wolverton where there was a railway church and a nice parsonage (*ironical cheers*). The Earl of Yarborough later referred to the Reverend Oldrid's speech and particularly his allusion to Sunday travelling.

> I cannot agree with the reverend gentleman in supposing that the cause of piety, religion and morality can be served by stopping railway travelling on Sundays, on the contrary I think that the cause of religion may be served by Sunday travelling, inasmuch as it is a great means of bringing the poor and others together on the only day which friends among the working people can meet those at a distance to exchange mutual expressions of regard; on which day the peasant father can exchange visits with his labouring son – to give advice and to exercise that wholesome paternal authority which is so desirable and should exist between parent and child (*applause*).

A ball in the Assembly Rooms was well attended, so too a dinner at the White Hart and a grand tea party at the Town Hall. Music and dancing prevailed in many inns in the town during the evening. The 'annihilation of time and space', by railway travel was complete and Boston and Lincolnshire were firmly established on the railway map.

The building of a permanent station had to wait until 1850; in the spring of that year Lincoln architect Henry Goddard drew up plans and in May a start was made on the construction of the new station, a little to the east of the temporary one. The station was opened in November 1850; it had distinctive iron canopies which enclosed the platform lines. A new refreshment room was included but not living accommodation for the station master and chief clerk, who had dwellings in West Street. A covered footbridge was erected at the station in 1864, as were new waiting rooms. In 1911 the original five-arch entrance of 1848 was abandoned in favour of a new entrance to the south, with a central booking office and covered access to the footbridge. New waiting rooms were added and the parcels office moved to the old entrance which had two of its arches demolished.

As the 1848 railway bridge over the River Witham was becoming an increasing hazard to navigation on the river, a new three span plate and box girder structure, designed by Richard Johnson, the GNR's Chief Engineer, was opened on 20th May, 1885.

A GNR class 'J16' locomotive under Low Street Bridge, Sleaford Junction, Boston in the early 1920s. Driver Bill Ely and Fireman J. Lighton are on the running plate.

Alan Turner

Chapter Five
Louth

Louth is situated at the point where the Wolds join the Marsh. There is no more dramatic prospect than that of the majestic spire of its parish church, St James, seen either from close by or glimpsed from several of the surrounding valleys or approach roads. Constitutionally Louth was one of the country's more peculiar boroughs from its incorporation by Edward VI, in 1551, until the Municipal Reform Act of 1835. In the charter of 1551 a Warden and six Assistants of the Town of Louth were appointed to govern both the town and the grammar school founded at the same time.

Louth owed its growth mainly to its position as an important market town at the junction of the marsh and the wolds. Some attempts were made to bring the industrial revolution to the town in the late 18th century, a canal was opened between Louth and Tetney Haven in 1770. In the early 19th century much activity was noted at the canal basin, 'Where a deal of business went on in coal and wool', also Adam Eve's wool and carpet factories and the boatyard. The town was too remote for a future based upon industry; the factories only employed a tiny proportion of the working population, a far greater number earned their living by serving the needs of the surrounding area.

Without doubt, after Boston and Grimsby, Louth was the most important place on the ELR. For many years Louth was the centre of railway operations in East Lincolnshire, it had motive power, engineering and signalling departments all based in the town. The railway was the largest employer in the district.

During the first two weeks in September 1845, a considerable number of surveyors and their assistants were busily engaged in different localities in the town trying to decide which would be suitable for the projected ELR. There were some objections from landowners, and, in one instance, some of the instruments being used by the surveyors were seized and held until a promise had been made not to repeat the trespass. A careful survey was being made of the traffic using roads entering the town. The majority feeling was in favour of the railway, influential citizens were exhorted to, 'speedily consult as to the best site for the station and how they may most effectively seize every fair advantage in connection with this movement to permanently benefit the town and posterity will rejoice at the enterprise.'

The foundation stone for the station was laid by Miss Charlotte Pye, the 16 year-old daughter of Henry Pye, a Director of the ELR company, who lived at 'The Cedars', St. Marys Lane, Louth, on 8th July, 1847.

> Thursday the 8th inst. being appointed for the depositing of the first stone of the foundation of the building by Miss Pye, of Louth, and the weather proving propitious, at about one o'clock persons of all grades began to move towards the station ground to witness the interesting ceremony and until about two the crowd continued to increase, when Miss Pye's carriage with several others arrived, containing many elegantly dressed ladies who were received by the Secretary and Engineer to the railway company and conducted to the immediate vicinity of the foundation. The arrangements on the occasion, which had been effected under the skilful superintendence of Mr John Dales, the builder of this place, seemed to

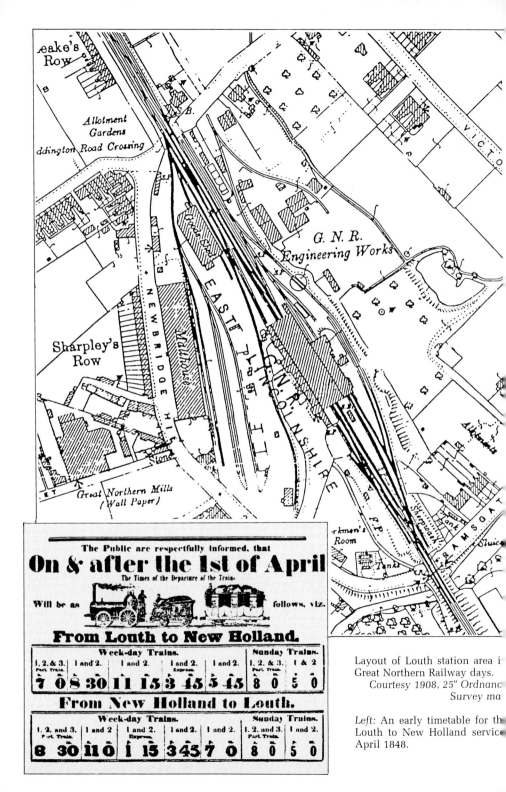

Layout of Louth station area in Great Northern Railway days.
Courtesy 1908, 25″ Ordnance Survey map

Left: An early timetable for the Louth to New Holland service, April 1848.

A coal wagon of LMS parentage being unloaded in Louth yard with local coal merchant Jackson ready to depart with a full quota.   *H. L. Howe*

Louth South signal box c.1887 with a Stirling 0–4–2 mixed traffic engine in the platform. This picture also gives a rare view of Louth's footbridge, soon to be replaced by a subway.
Author's Collection

An LNER lorry loaded up and being refuelled at Louth goods shed during the severe winter of 1947.
H. L. Howe

constitute the principal object of interest and received the entire approval of the assembled many. After Mr Kirk, the original contractor for the building of the stations on the line, had announced the completion of preparations for the ceremony, Miss Pye, leaning on the arm of her father, accompanied by Mrs J.H. Short, descended a flight of steps leading into the trench, when Miss Pye gracefully handled a handsome trowel newly prepared for this occasion, and having distributed the mortar along the foundation, the stone was lowered into its resting place, and received from Miss Pye the adjusting tap of an elegant mahogany mallet, after which three hearty cheers were given. Mr Pye then delivered a short address.

After the ceremony upwards of 60 of the principal individuals of the assembly adjourned to the booth erected in the grounds and partook of the refreshments provided. In the evening a dinner party comprising some of the officials and others were entertained at the 'Kings Head'. The trowel used by Miss Pye at the ceremony still survives in the Louth Museum. Silver, with an ivory handle, it bears an engraving of the station and a description of the ceremony on one side. On the reverse there is a coat of arms and a list of persons involved with the construction of the railway, as follows:

George Hussey Packe, Chairman of the Board of Directors
John Fowler, Engineer in Chief
Henry Fowler, Resident Engineer
Weightman and Hadfield, Architects
Holway and Harwood, of Spilsby and Pye and Waite of Louth, Solicitors
William Heaford Daubney, of Great Grimsby
John Deniston

By October the centre part and the side wings of the station building were erected and ready for roofing. Rapid progress was being made on a large warehouse to the north of the station measuring 204 ft by 64 ft. The gatehouse at the intersection of Brackenborough Road was finished and being used as an office. A month later the station roof was almost completed, a gasworks was finished and ready to operate, and piles were being driven for the foundation of the engine shed opposite the eastern face of the station and on the site of a considerable brick yard.

The completed section was a handsome neo-Jacobean style building with curved red-brick stone-capped gables, a balustraded roof with linked chimney stacks and a superb stone round arched *porte-cochère* with Renaissance details. The platform side was, unusually, constructed in white brick. A station master's house was added a few years after the station was built, very much in sympathy with the main structure but of a more traditional style. A single-storey building was added to the north end, and two stone arched doorways appeared on either side of the *porte-cochère*; a small kiosk-type room in the same style was added to the north of the northern door.

Soon after the opening of the complete line, the GNR and ELR were accused of casting an injurious slight on Louth in the arrangement of their market trains. It had been ordered that after 1st May, 1849, market trains for Boston were to leave Gainsborough and Louth at 7 am calling at all intermediate stations and returning from Boston at 4.30 pm, every Wednesday and Saturday. First, second and third class day tickets were available entitling passengers to return the same day on any train other than the express.

Louth regarded its market to be of equal importance and petitioned that it should be granted similar privileges particularly as its market day coincided with that of Boston (Wednesday).

At about the same time a petition was signed by a great number of people and presented to both Houses of Parliament, against the trade in, 'seduction and prostitution'. The feeling was that legislation had become necessary because the facilities for travelling afforded by the railways had resulted in increasing female immorality. 'Young females, 15 to 20 years old, are watched on the approach of London trains and by lying and subtlety are led away to their ruin'.

Changes that occurred at Louth in the next few years included the destruction by a fierce gale, on 28th May, 1860, of the original wooden goods shed. This was replaced by a large brick built building of typical GNR architectural style.

In January 1879, a temperance refreshment room, 'of ample dimensions and complete proportions and appliances', was opened on the station by the Holy Trinity Temperance Association.

A bay was constructed on the up side to coincide with the opening of the Mablethorpe branch and for the use of branch trains. The south end was resignalled and the South box built, and was completed by October 1887. On 13th January the following year a passenger subway was opened to replace the original footbridge. As a way of crossing the line, this was unique in Lincolnshire stations. The reason for this is not clear but it may be that vision from the new South box was restricted by the footbridge.

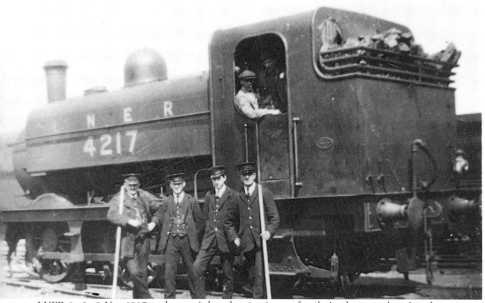

LNER 0–6–0 No. 4217 and crew (plus shunters) pose for their photograph at Louth yard in 1928. *Paul King*

A good view from Firsby footbridge (looking south) showing the unusual crossing gate arrangements and the Skegness line curving off to the left just beyond the crossover. The right hand side crossover served the Spilsby line (25th May, 1970).   *G. H. Brown*

A view of Firsby station frontage and portico looking north on 16th September, 1962.
G. H. Brown

Chapter Six
Firsby Junction

Two independent companies, the Spilsby and Firsby and the Wainfleet and Firsby joined the East Lincolnshire line at Firsby. By 1880 Skegness had become a popular seaside report attracting over 106,000 excursion passengers to the town during that year. As all excursion trains had to reverse at Firsby the installation of the south curve was deemed essential. Powers obtained in 1874 had lapsed but it was nevertheless resolved to purchase the land required and construct the curve. The line was laid double track on a 10 chains radius curve. The construction of an overbridge at the eastern end of the curve enabled a level crossing to be abolished. Two new signal boxes for the junction were built at Firsby South and East. Construction (although already completed) was authorised by an Act on 18th July, 1881.

Firsby was an important junction and its station building, although situated in the middle of nowhere, advertised its importance. The station remained much the same over the years. Changes did occur however. The excellent 3-arm signal shown in earlier photographs was replaced by a concrete post on the down platform carrying three small arms referred to by the LNER as 'miniature'. The lowest of the three was labelled 'Signal miniature down main to Spilsby line'. In 1880 there were no gates between the up main line and the Skegness line. The inner home signal was further from the platform end. Perhaps it was road widening that determined its later position and also gave the opportunity to install the double set of crossing gates which folded over each other when closed, an arrangement I have not seen elsewhere.

The original signal box comprised of three bays of brickwork but the box was extended by a further bay at the crossing end in 1927. This was to accommodate a new Saxby Duplex frame replacing the original Stevens frame. The new frame was installed at the back of the signal cabin in order to facilitate the changeover. This meant that the Firsby signalman worked with his back to the trains.

Electrically operated points (one of the earliest examples of track circuits and motor operated points) replaced the East Junction signal box on 9th October, 1927, the same day as the new frame in Firsby box was brought into use.

Because of its isolated position newspaper reports about Firsby tend to be few and far between and were included in the reports of the Spilsby correspondent. The *Stamford Mercury*, 22nd August, 1885, reported that waiting rooms were being added to the up platform. Hitherto there had been no accommodation offered and complaining passengers had to endure the cold piercing winds while waiting for trains. It also remarked that the footbridge, erected some years earlier, had been a great boon in the prevention of accidents.

On 6th October, 1890, an accident occurred to the Spilsby engine, on its way to bring up the Skegness market train. On approaching Firsby the engine, with all the signals against it, attempted to enter the station but instead ran into a dead siding at the end of the signal box, smashing the stop block and throwing the engine off the rails. The signal box narrowly escaped destruction, the signalman, seeing the engine's determined approach, fled the box. Amazingly no one was hurt and another locomotive was procured to work the traffic.

Gordon Brown wrote a vivid description of the station to accompany his two views on *pages 38 and 42*.

The photo looking north shows a good view of the approach to the yard and goods shed, also a small building which, I think, was a checking office. The projection at the distant (north) end of the building was the station master's house; his garden gate is by the corner of the building. His front door opened into the down platform and bore a cast iron notice 'Residence'. The near end projection was also a dwelling house, occupied before the war by one of the station staff, Mr Chapman I believe. His garden/back yard was enclosed by the wall at the extreme right of the picture. The 'hut' behind the stone portico was a temporary office which appeared sometime after World War II. It had disappeared by the time the second photo was taken. In the latter the shoring up of the roof will be noted – this was part of the general waiting room which opened off the booking hall, its floor had been rotten for many years. Next to the general waiting room, nearest the camera, was the refreshment room which was independently run. I do not recall when it went out of business. For a time, in GNR days, before her marriage my mother used to work there, and used to tell of the brisk business done, and the crowds using the Wednesday Boston market train, and also the Spilsby line on Monday, Spilsby market day. This would be World War I or thereabouts. Also before World War II, Mrs H. Penson worked there for a while before her marriage. One of her jobs, I recall, was to wander along the platform selling chocolate etc. from a shoulder hung tray while trains waited to leave; no drinks though, disposable cartons had not been invented then. The refreshment room itself was quite well equipped, the tea and coffee machines were heated from the station gas supply, as was the washing up water, quite modern!

The main entrance to the station was the door beneath the portico, which gave on to the L-shaped booking hall. Directly opposite was the door to the booking office. The passenger turned left then right along the 'L' of the booking hall: to the left was the door to the general waiting room, to the right the ticket issuing windows, ahead the arch leading to the platform. On display in the booking hall were boards carrying packs of handbills giving details of all sorts of services on offer, with the invitation to 'please take one'. In practice the main entrance was not used all that much, except for parcels traffic, for at the far end of the building seen in the south facing photograph, behind the enclosure wall of the dwelling house, there was a wide entrance gate for mails and newspapers, and an alcove convenient for parking a mail van.

Most of the passengers from the west (Great Steeping) direction used the entrance to the down platform and it was here that the ticket collector used to stand more often than not. Passengers from the eastern direction would use the handgate and the level crossing. Passengers from either direction would tend to use the handgate and level crossing for access to or from the up side and the Skegness bay, and almost everyone wishing to buy tickets walked along the down platform and entered the booking hall that way. So the elegant entrance failed to receive the honour due. Again looking at the south facing photograph, beyond the station building is seen the garden hedge of the house at the extreme end of the down platform, its chimney visible above the tree. Between the wars this house was occupied by Mr Barford, for many years an important member of the station staff, whose official title was either ticket collector or yard foreman, I believe, anyway he certainly did both jobs. It was he who persuaded driver Barwick to let me, then still quite young, ride on the Spilsby engine as it ran-round. I can remember it well, it was an Ivatt 4–4–0 that week.

Trains on the Boston to Skegness line not stopping at Firsby station travelled round the tight curve and avoided the station. Trains between Grimsby and Skegness were diverted along the single line on to the Skegness branch. They had to set back at the station from the up road to the Skegness line as there were no facing points. So the actual turnout facing the train as it set back had no facing point lock, being installed for shunting movements only. This applied to both possible routes, the crossover up main line to the Skegness bay, or the crossover up main to down main. Before World War II trains were cheerfully set back over the unlocked points, usually into the Skegness bay. In due course tests were carried out to scotch or clamp the points. The scotch did not hold the points securely so the clamp had to be used. The result of this new practice was that setting back over the main crossover to the down platform became the favoured route, as it was not so far for the man with the clamp to walk as the alternative route at the far end of the station. A request was made on several occasions for facing points, (a double slip in the through road) but this was refused on the grounds that the curve was too sharp. However, it was nothing like as sharp at the south curve. The likelihood is that the need for a two-arm signal (up inner home) at the platform end would have been very difficult for a driver to see, with the risk of a mishap due to excessive speed.

The triangle was also used regularly for turning engines. This was brought about by the removal of the turntable and turning triangle at Skegness, and because of the limited turning facilities at Mablethorpe. (The Mablethorpe branch diverged from the East Lincolnshire line north of Firsby at Willough-by Junction.)

Engines were turned at Firsby as follows: the engine would travel on the up main line to Firsby South where it would reverse direction and be switched on to the down main line round the curve to Firsby East. The engine would reverse again on to the single line leading back to the station, either being turned into the bay platform or over the down road crossover into the down platform.

Branch trains operated between Skegness and Firsby making connections with main line services at the junction. These trains arrived and departed from the bay platform. When the engine had been uncoupled it ran to Firsby North where it crossed to the up line, thence round the triangle, rejoining its train at the opposite end and with the engine turned in the manoeuvre.

Engines arriving from Mablethorpe for Boston at the up platform tender first would uncouple, turn on the triangle and rejoin their train.

Some trains from Boston to Skegness stopped at Firsby. After arrival at the down platform the engine was uncoupled and ran to Firsby North, it would then follow the procedure of the branch line engines, but did not go into the bay. The train departed along the single line and joined the down line of the Skegness branch. The down platform at Firsby was bi-directional, being the arrival and departure platform for the Spilsby branch trains.

Trains booked to stop at Firsby and requiring the engine to be turned were allowed 10 minutes for the movement. On Sundays and Bank Holidays, when many specials were worked into Skegness and Mablethorpe, the engines were detached from their trains on arrival, coupled together and worked back to Firsby, tender first, to be turned on the triangle. Sometimes as many as eight engines were coupled together and turned.

Mr George Cargill, who worked at both Firsby signal boxes, said that in 1949 there could be up to 100 movements in a day, increasing to about 170 a day at weekends.

As well as dealing with branch line traffic and summer excursion traffic, the East Lincolnshire line dealt with goods and passenger traffic working, from such places as Kings Cross, Peterborough and Boston through to Grimsby and back. Perhaps worth mentioning are the 8.30 am and the 4.30 pm down all-stations Peterborough to Grimsby services, both of which were New England 'Atlantic' turns. The engine of the former came up with the 2.00 pm express connecting at Peterborough, and the latter returned on the 9.00 pm up mail to Peterborough. (The third New England 'Atlantic' turn came down with the 4.30 am mail and newspaper train, returning with the 10.00 am express – the main London train of the day.) The expresses in the down direction at 7.00 pm and 9.45 pm were worked by Immingham GCR engines.

Goods traffic closed on 7th December, 1964 and the closure of the East Lincolnshire line on 5th October, 1970 saw the end of Firsby station. At first the points at Firsby South were clamped for through running to Skegness, eventually the line was altered to plain track and a 15 mph speed restriction applied on the severe curve. This situation still exists at the south junction.

Firsby's huge and beautiful goods shed (80 ft by 100 ft) has survived the station; built of brick it has simple recessed blank arches on its south and north sides, and a series of superb round arched windows, matching those of the water tower, on the east and west sides. Firsby was a place where one felt the contrast between man and nature because of their close proximity. The station stood like a mansion without a garden: a train passed through, its sound giving way to the sound of sparrows and circling skylarks; today only the birds remain, the trains have gone, so too has the station.

Firsby station entrance looking south, May 1970.   *G. H. Brown*

Chapter Seven
Willoughby and Alford

WILLOUGHBY

Eighteenth century travellers in the Lincolnshire marshes found the villages to be straggling settlements of mud huts, with only the principal farmhouses constructed of brick and tile. By the 19th century Willoughby appears to have become one of the problem parishes of the Willoughby d'Eresby estate. The farms had their lands scattered and intermingled over a large area, and most of the farmhouses were situated far from their fields in the centre of the village, 'amongst the public houses and beer shops, it is the destruction of many farmers and engenders bad habits in their men'. However, by 1848, much building was being carried out and, in 1856, the Directory describes Willoughby as a neat 'village'.

In 1887 a great change was effected at the station due to the opening of the line to Sutton-on-Sea. Formerly the only accommodation for passengers had been afforded by a portion of the station master's house. This was replaced by a new and larger station, 'with well appointed waiting rooms which will be greatly appreciated in cold and stormy weather'. The new station signal box was described as 'elevated', and 'at night when lighted up will be a conspicuous land mark'. However popular the facilities were with travellers, these were tempered by criticism of the delays caused by the level crossing, 'people riding and driving horses experience all the inconvenience of a level crossing, farmers and other businessmen complaining of the time they are kept waiting at the gates'.

The original station at Willoughby was situated on the south side of the road crossing adjacent to the station master's house. In order to facilitate the construction of the junction with the Sutton and Willoughby Railway, land was purchased from the Lord Willoughby d'Ersby estate to the north of the crossing, the work included the building of a new station. Contractor James Dickinson of St Albans began to level out the way beyond the junction in June 1885. The old station closed on 4th October, 1886. The new station at Willoughby had three faces, the up platform being an island.

As the station was approached from the village a right turn brought one on to the bay platform and to the main station buildings; these consisted of parcels office, station master's office, ticket office, general waiting room, ladies' waiting room, porters' room, toilets. These were all on the up main and branch bay platform. On the down platform was a ladies' general waiting room. Two new signal boxes were built, at the station and at the junction. The Station box was sited behind the down platform close by the footbridge and crossing. The Junction signal box beyond the north end of the island platform, was a 'points box', operated by the station staff for movement on and off the main line as well as into and out of the branch bay. Branch trains worked in and out of the back platform.

The signalling tablet instruments were Tyer's No. 7 types rather than the more usual No. 6 type; the former, although more modern, were prone to failure resulting in the signalman getting 'two half-slides' (a malfunction of the tablet equipment). The 1912 Appendix stated that the box was 'Open only for passing branch traffic'.

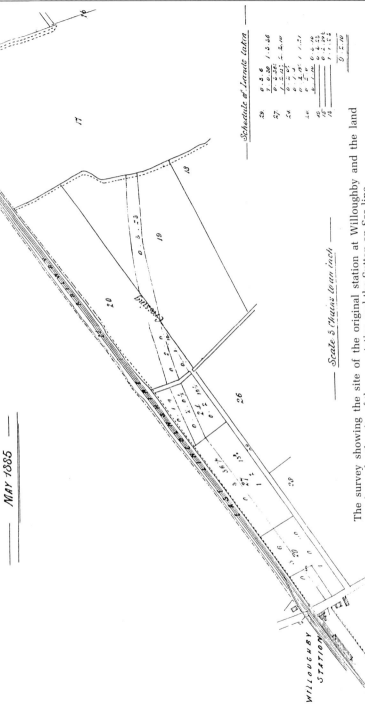

The survey showing the site of the original station at Willoughby and the land purchases for the site of the new station and the Sutton-on-Sea line.

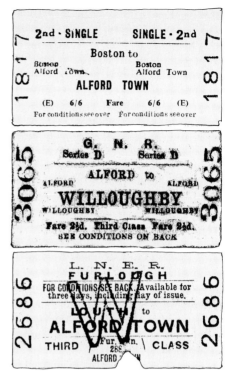

Lady porter Lydia Hay, employed at Willoughby station during World War Two. *Bob Riddington*

Willoughby station staff, *c.* 1920. *Back row* (*L to R*): Tom Thorndike, signalman; unknown; Mr. Kime; Wally Chapman, coal merchant; Mr. Fawcett, platelayer. *Front row*: Harry Reed, signalman; Alf Jacklin, porter; Mr. Kew; Harry Hammond, station master; two unknown lad porters; Ted Newcome, porter. *Author's Collection*

Lines through the station were level and straight, and there was a small goods yard which included a goods shed and end loading bank on the up side south of the crossing. On the down side were two sidings, one used for coal traffic; private owner wagons belonging to the local coal merchant were marked, 'M. Chapman'. Towards the end of the line's life coal was also carted by Scupholm of Wainfleet. A roughly constructed loading bank was situated at the south end of the down siding used for milk traffic. This served the Clover Dairy factory, which sent out milk daily by train until the 1950s. In the early days milk was despatched in GNR bogie milk vans. The 1937 Working Timetable showed that the 3.15 pm 'No. 2 braked empties', called at Willoughby to detach empty milk vans, while the mid-afternoon Grimsby to Peterborough train collected a milk van here. Milk was sent to Hull Paragon in a van picked up by the 4.19 pm Grimsby–Peterborough passenger train – geographically an eccentric movement.

Two important trains were the two Cleethorpes–Kings Cross Buffet expresses calling at Willoughby at 7.32 am and 9.50 am. These returned at night at 7.05 pm and 9.35 pm, but the latter did not stop at Willoughby; at least it was not booked to do so, although Bob Riddington recalled an occasion when it did. He was visiting his friend Len Smith, who was on duty at the signal box. Despite having a clear road, the train hauled by ex-GCR 4–6–0 *Valour* stopped near the box; the driver was in an agitated state and thought he had hit something leaving Burgh station. He said he would move the train off the crossing and then inspect the front of the engine. The men took a handlamp and to their dismay discovered a pretty gory mess liberally plastered over the buffer beam. Len Smith rang through to Burgh signal box, his demeanour changing from anxiety to jocularity as the conversation developed. Apparently *Valour* had run over a large container of what can only be described as cat food. The container was part of a consignment for a circus performer who lived between Burgh and Skegness, and who kept tigers on his property!

On Saturdays in the summer the local service between Willoughby and Mablethorpe would start from the down the main line platform instead of the bay, because of the large amount of parcels and luggage mainly due to the holiday traffic.

Goods traffic ceased at this station on 2nd May, 1966, passenger traffic remaining until the line's closure on 5th October, 1970.

ALFORD

The predominant feature of the town of Alford is the 19th century brick and tile works, a result of the town's modest commercial expansion and local importance brought about by the arrival of the railway. Industry in the town during this time was strongly related to agriculture, agricultural implement making, tanning, corn milling, brewing, ropemaking and brick manufacturing being among the most important. The thatched manor house and a number of cottages roofed in the same material remain as isolated representatives of what, in the 18th century, was the universal roofing material in the town.

A northbound 'grimy' class 'B1' 4−6−0 No. 61111 pauses at Willoughby in the summer of 1963 with a passenger train.   *Bob Riddington*

Willoughby station looking north, possibly soon after the opening of the new station in 1887.   *Author's Collection*

The station building, similar to that at Firsby in style, had a three arch portico entrance letting into a passageway leading out on to the platform. The passageway contained the entrance to a large parcels office and the ticket window and its corresponding office. Between these offices and the station master's residence at the southern end of the building was the ladies' waiting room. Turning right on the platform, one found the general waiting room, a store room, the station master's office and another residence, the one time domicile of Mr Hardwick, a lorry driver and one time porter. Platforms were opposite each other protected by an overall roof, (replaced by a canopy after World War II); both the station buildings and the signal box, situated near the road crossing at the north end of the station, were on the up side of the running lines. The position of the signal box caused some heavy lever movements due to its distance from the points it operated.

Behind the platform on the down side was a running line and a refuge siding for 44 wagons. The station yard had a loading dock, a goods shed, which could take 9 wagons, and contained Harrisons grain store in its upper storey. This shed and a 15 ton crane were blown up during World War II causing the death of the only person killed in Alford during the hostilities, shunt horse driver Bush, who was on fire watch at the time. The pointwork in the yard was quite elaborate and shunting could take place on both sides of the running line.

During World War II, Alford signalmen Jack Whitelam and Frank Gooding were supplemented by Fred Bullock, who had reached retirement age as a signalman but was offered a porter-signalman's job. This meant he worked a half shift, the other two men working full shifts. The shifts ran from 4.30 am to 12 noon, 12 to 3.30 pm and 3.30 to 'finish'. In March 1953 the manning of Alford signal box was increased to three shifts to accommodate the High Dyke-Frodingham ironstone trains and the Nottinghamshire, Colwick based, coal trains and their respective empties. Trains were directed over the ELR because of the necessity of reversals at Lincoln and Barnetby on the old GCR route. Alford box at this time was dealing with 60 to 70 trains, passenger and freight, every 24 hours. Station masters recalled by Frank Gooding include Messrs Berry, Saggers, Walker and Savage; Clerks, Dick Enderby, Les Stephenson, Ken Smith and during World War II Mary Briggs, Mary Margrave and Ena Hardwick; Porters, Arthur Lowe and Alf Robinson; Motor Drivers, Billy Hardwick and Bill Atkin; Shunt horse driver Bush; Signalmen, Frank Gooding, Jack Whitelam, Fred Bullock, Arthur Bullock, Len Tabor and Ivor Smith, rest day relief. Platelayers were, Hedley Sizer (ganger) Arthur Dennis (sub ganger) Jack Bly, Arthur Sizer and Ted Leverton. Alford Town station buildings have survived the closure, on 5th October, 1970 and, with the goods yard, form part of an industrial estate served by a road with the appropriate (?) name, Beeching Way!

Chapter Eight
Intermediate Stations

North of Boston the line passed over a series of water courses, the most notable being Maude Foster Drain; a signal box of this name stood on the west side of the line and controlled the gates on the Coningsby Road. The first station was at Sibsey, a small village situated on the Horncastle Road. A 1909 plan shows a four road goods yard facing Boston but by the mid-1920s this had been extended to seven roads and, eventually, eight. Extra land was purchased at Sibsey by the GNR in 1896, 1912 and 1914, no doubt to facilitate the extension of the yard to cope with the increasing potato and sugar beet traffic. Passenger services were withdrawn in September 1961 and freight in 1964.

Old Leake was next along the line boasting only an inn apart from the station, the village itself was situated to the east of the line. Originally named, 'Hob Hole', then renamed, 'Leake and Wrangle', it became, 'Old Leake and Wrangle' in 1849 and finally, 'Old Leake' in 1852. Passenger closure was on 17th September, 1956, goods continuing until total closure on 15th June, 1964.

Eastville station was set in the middle of the village, with two long sidings on the up side; on the down side was a small goods yard, a warehouse and a long headshunt. The level crossing and signal box were at the north end of the parallel platforms, the main station building being on the down platform. Large amounts of sugar beet were moved here in block loads, all hand forked into the waiting wagons. Freight was always a more important trade than passengers. The village and parish of Eastville was a new creation after the draining of the East Fen in the early 1800s. The ELR had difficulty with the quaking peatlands, using alternative layers of faggots, peat and clay to form a low embankment on which to lay the line. The station closed on 11th September, 1961.

Little Steeping station buildings were on the down platform and the signal box was on the up side, close by a minor road which connected Little Steeping with Great Steeping to the north. It closed to passengers on 11th September, 1961, goods and complete closure following on 15th June, 1964.

Burgh-le-Marsh had parallel platforms, all the main offices, goods shed, small crane, large cattle dock and signal box on the up (east) side. A level crossing immediately north of the station crossed the main road which led to Burgh (two miles away) and eventually Skegness. There was a long refuge siding here capable of holding 80 wagons.

Between Burgh and Aby were Willoughby (3½ miles) and Alford Town (6 miles); Aby a further 3 miles up the line served the two hamlets of Aby and Claythorpe and was situated on a skew level crossing. When opened in 1848 it was named 'Claythorpe', later changed to 'Aby for Claythorpe' on 1st November, 1885. Aby had a goods shed and was the first goods yard to close on 11th September, 1961; passenger services here ceased on the same day.

Authorpe was a mile further on and situated west of the hamlet of the same name. The signal box was opened as required usually under the care of the Aby signalman. It too lost its passenger services on 11th September, 1961. Goods and final closure came on 30th March, 1964.

Continued on page 93

Sibsey signal box. This photograph gives a good indication of the flat nature of the landscape through which the ELR ran, and also the straightness of the line.

Alan Turner

LNER class 'J11' 0–6–0 No. 64372 passes through Boston station heading towards the East Lincolnshire line with the morning goods in 1958.   *Les Perrin*

A 'Britannia' class 4–6–2 No. 70038 *Robin Hood*, with the 8.32 am Cleethorpes–Kings Cross service seen here at Boston in July 1962.   *Les Perrin*

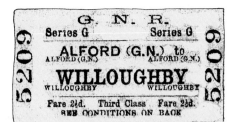

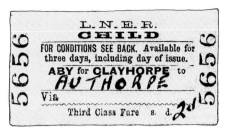

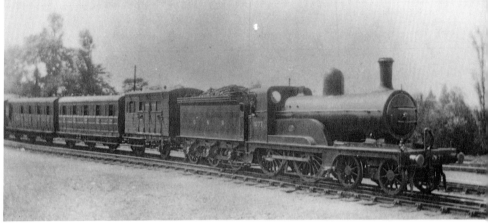

Class 'D4' 4–4–0 No. 1077 at Boston in 1921. This engine was rebuilt to class 'D3' by the LNER in 1923 and withdrawn in 1937. _J. F. Vickery_

Maude Foster signal box was a block post (with 12 levers) – the first out of Boston on the East Lincolnshire line. _H. B. Priestley_

A good view of Sibsey station and signal box photographed in September 1958.
H. B. Priestley

Sibsey station, signal box and station staff. This picture gives some feeling of the remoteness associated with many stations on the East Lincolnshire line.
Author's Collection

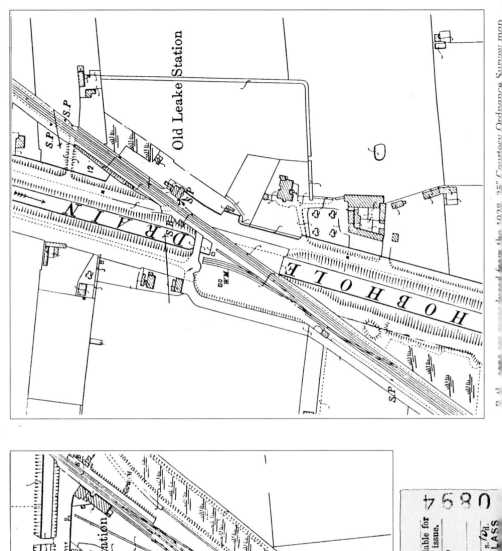

Old Leake Station

DRAIN

HOBHOLE

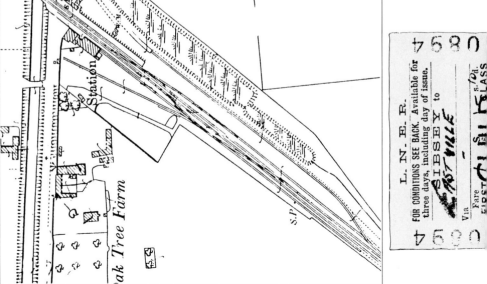

Oak Tree Farm

Station

A good indication of the rural situation of Old Leake station, as seen in March 1967.
H. B. Priestley

A railway carriage being moved from Old Leake station by Messrs Rundles of Bolingbroke. Jack Rundles' steam wagon was made in 1920 by the Yorkshire Engine Company, Leeds. *Alan Turner*

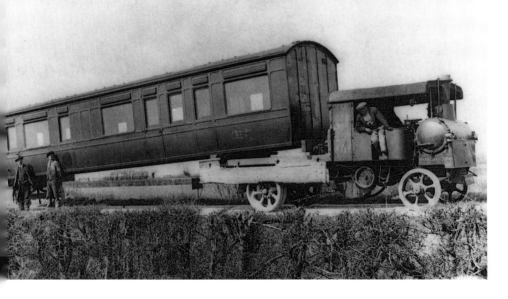

A train approaches Eastville station. Note the large goods shed and the splendid somersault signal. *Author's Collection*

A DMU approaches the site of Eastville station in March 1967. Both platforms have been demolished and the line to the goods shed lifted. *H. B. Priestley*

A splendid view of Bellwater Junction, the loneliest signal box on the GNR. It was at this point that the 'new line' from Conningsby Junction joined the East Lincolnshire line (seen in August 1970).

Peter Grey

A DMU passes through a neat Little Steeping station, the goods yard still in active use at the time. *H. B. Priestley*

The scene had changed dramatically by March 1967: the platforms had been demolished and there was a general air of desolation about the place. *H. B. Priestley*

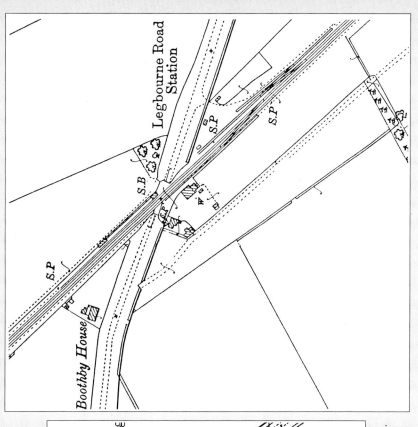

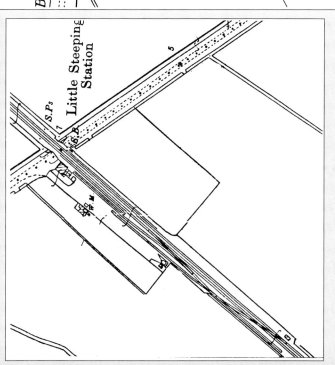

Both maps are reproduced from the 1928, 25" Ordnance Survey map.

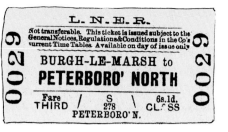

A very fine 1931 photo of a 4–4–0 class 'D3' locomotive No. 4308 leaving Firsby and heading for the Conningsby line. *J. E. Kite*

Class 'B1' 4–6–0 No. 61240 *Harry Hinchcliffe* at the East box, Firsby Junction, returning from Skegness light engine and heading towards Boston, at about 2.50 pm on 1st July, 1964. *G. H. Brown*

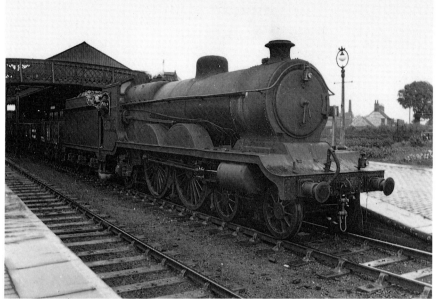

Ex-GCR class 'C4' locomotive No. 2909 works a freight train through Firsby station, c.1950. No. 2909 was built in 1905, shedded at both Boston and Immingham and was withdrawn in November 1950. *Alan Turner*

Ex-GNR class 'C1' No. 4409 on a Skegness–Kings Cross train, leaving Firsby South in 1945. The finials on the signals were later removed by British Railways for some unexplained reason. *T. G. Hepburn*

On 11th July, 1959, class 'B1' 4−6−0 No. 61390, with the 12.46 pm from Grimsby to Peterborough stands alongside the 2.18 pm DMU to Skegness, at the southern end of Firsby station. *H. B. Priestley*

Class 'V2' 2−6−2 No. 4829 with a heavy train of naval personnel on leave at Firsby station. The 'V2' had worked an early morning local to Grimsby from Peterborough on this day in 1945. *T. G. Hepburn*

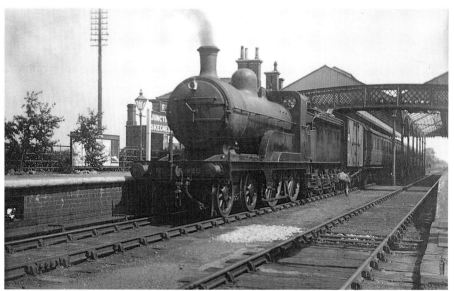

In 1934 4−4−0 class 'D3' locomotive No. 4304 stands by the old 'Firsby Junction for Wainfleet, Skegness and Spilsby' station sign. This was replaced in the 1950s with a British Railways tin sign bearing the brief legend 'Firsby'.   *J. E. Kite*

An early diesel unit enters Firsby station from the south on 16th July, 1959. Note the three arm 'miniature' signal which controlled Skegness, Boston and Spilsby trains.
                                                                    H. B. Priestley

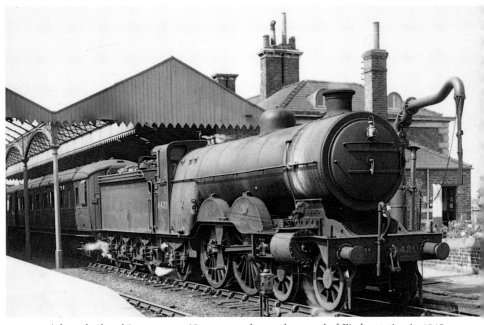

A large-boilered Ivatt 4−4−2 No. 4421 at the northern end of Firsby station in 1945.
T. G. Hepburn

Class 'D10' 4−4−0 *The Earl of Kerry*, built for the Great Central Railway in 1913, heads a Peterborough−Grimsby local at Firsby in 1946. The engine still carries the abbreviated 'NE' wartime livery of the LNER.　　　　　*T. G. Hepburn*

Ex-LMS 2−6−0 'Crab' No. 42823, seen on an excursion train at Firsby South. Note again the finials have been removed from the splendid bracket signal.   *N. E. Stead*

Class 'C12' locomotive No. 4548 calls at Firsby station with a Louth train via Sutton-on-Sea. There is also a good view of the overall roof at Firsby.   *T. G. Hepburn*

A fine period picture of Burgh station and staff in GNR days. This view looking south.
Author's Collection

By the time this photograph was taken in 1959 the signs on the signal box, seats and
the station proclaimed 'Burgh-le-Marsh'. *H. B. Priestley*

A view of Burgh-le-Marsh crossing on 2nd March, 1972. The crossing box controlled traffic passing along the road to Skegness. *R. B. Wilkinson*

The goods shed at Burgh-le-Marsh at present houses the Lincolnshire Railway Museum operated by Alan Turner and his family. Alan's father was a signalman on the line and his photograph appears beneath the 'Contents' list at the beginning of this book. *Author's Collection*

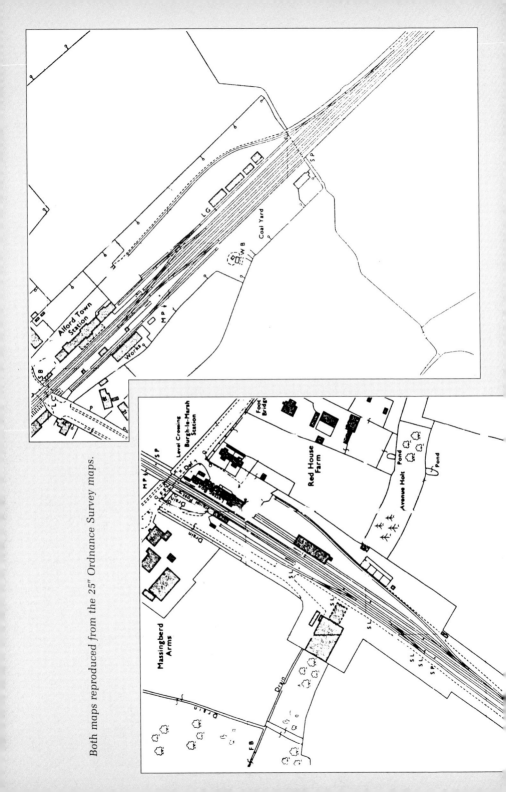

Both maps reproduced from the 25" Ordnance Survey maps.

A good view of Willoughby station showing the main line to Grimsby and the Mablethorpe bay to the right. The signal box beyond the platform end controlled traffic on and off the Mablethorpe branch. *H. B. Priestley*

A close-up of the Mablethorpe branch box and junction. A Brush 'Type 2' No. D5820 comes off the branch with a special bound for Sheffield in 1969. *John Vaughan*

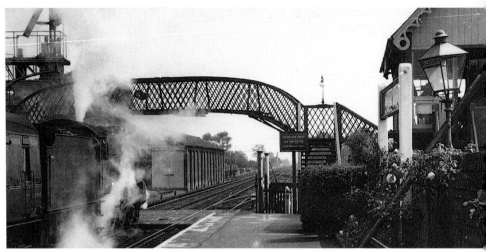

An evocative photo of Willoughby, including somersault signal, footbridge, gas light and well-tended gardens for which the station won many awards; seen here in July 1959.
H. B. Priestley

An interesting view showing the last of the old Stirling 2–4–0s No. 3814 shunting at Willoughby. No. 3814 was shedded at Louth when it was withdrawn from service in November 1927.
J. E. Kite

A fine view of Willoughby station signal box and neatly sculptured hedges. *Bob Riddington*

LNER class 'C12' locomotive No. 67384 arriving in the bay platform at Willoughby station with a passenger train from Louth. Further examples of the station staff's gardening skills are evident in this photo.   *R. J. Buckley*

A large-boilered Atlantic class 'C1' No. 4420 enters Willoughby station with a Grimsby–Peterborough train in the summer of 1945.   *T. G. Hepburn*

An Immingham class 'B1' 4–6–0 steams into Alford Town station on 11th July, 1959.
The overall roof had by this time been replaced by the ugly looking canopy.

H. B. Priestley

A lovely photograph of an ex-GCR class 'O4' locomotive passing through Alford Town
station with a Frodingham–Whitemoor freight train in 1936. *Bob Riddington*

The entrance to Alford Town station which bore a family resemblance to that at Firsby. The road is now aptly named 'Beeching Way'

Author's Collection

An LNER class 'J6' 0−6−0 passes through Aby station on an up goods in 1939.

Ivor Smith

Another view of Aby signal box being approached by an ex-GCR class 'B4' loco-motive No. 6098 with an up empty-coaches train in 1939.

Ivor Smith

Not a particularly clear photograph but it does contain a rare view of Aby goods shed,
c.1910.   *Alan Turner*

A neat and well kept Aby station, as
seen in 1963.   *D. Thompson*

An unknown signalma[n]
poses for his photogra[ph]
at Aby box. This may ha[ve]
been the shortest name [of]
any signal box in t[he]
country?   *Alan Turn[er]*

A   passenger   tra[in]
approaches Aby station [in]
GNR   days.   Note   t[he]
spectacle   low   down   [of]
the signal post.
      Author's Collecti[on]

Authorpe station looking north in 1963.   *D. Thompson*

Authorpe station looking south. Note the staggered platforms situated either side of the crossing gates.   *D. Thompson*

Legbourne Road station with the track partially dismantled, 2nd December, 1970.   R. B. Wilkinson

Legbourne Road signal box seen just prior to its demolition in December 1970.   R. B. Wilkinson

Legbourne Road crossing in 1963. The station is now restored and houses a collection of railwayania. D. Thompson

The elegant Mablethorpe Junction box; at this point the Mablethorpe branch left the East Lincolnshire line rejoining it at Willoughby Junction.
R. B. Wilkinson

Wragby Junction, where the Louth to Bardney branch left the East Lincolnshire line. An ex-GCR class 'D9' locomotive passes with a southbound passenger train. *P. Grey*

The northern end of Louth station photographed on 11th July, 1959.   *H. B. Priestley*

The elegant frontage of Louth station with some busy passenger activity in July 1959.
H. B. Priestley

Class '31' No. 113 delivers a vanfit of fibre glass to ABM, Louth, in April 1979. The maltings behind the goods shed dominated the station area for many years; the crossing is Keddington Road.   *M. Roughley*

A class '31' locomotive alongside Louth north signal box at Keddington Road crossing with the station and goods shed visible beyond the gates, 25th April, 1979.
                                                                            M. Roughley

An ex-GNR class 'C1' locomotive awaits departure with an up train from Louth in the 1930s. *Author's Collection*

Although photographed in June 1950; the horse is still being used for shunting at Louth station; a scene that could have been pre-1900! *Mike Black*

The Louth–Grimsby coaching stock standing in the bay at the northern end of Louth station on 16th May, 1954.   *Author's Collection*

Ex-GCR class 'A5' 4–6–2T No. 9817, shunts wagons in Louth station on 18th May, 1949 while class 'C12' 4–4–2T No. 7359 simmers quietly behind the water column.
                                                                                                           P. H. Wells

A 1950s view of Louth goods shed taken from the maltings with plenty of clutter for the modeller to observe. Immingham class 'J11' 0–6–0 No. 64323 hurries past on the main line with a northbound mineral train.
H. L. Howe

Louth based class 'D2' 4–4–0 No. 4383 at the north end of Louth station on 9th May, 1946.
H. C. Casserley

Fotherby Halt, seen in the 1960s. Note that steps were provided to assist passengers on and off trains by this time (*compared with photograph below*).   D. Thompson

A railmotor departs Utterby Halt. Notice the short low platforms built especially for the railmotors.   *D. N. Robinson Collection*

A fine period view of Ludborough station showing the low railmotor platform. The main platforms at Ludborough were staggered each side of the crossing gates. The splendid goods shed still survives. *Author's Collection*

Ludborough station with a GNR class 'E3', No. 294, arriving from the north, c.1910. By April 1912 No. 294 was the last surviving class 'E3' and was withdrawn that year. *Alan Turner*

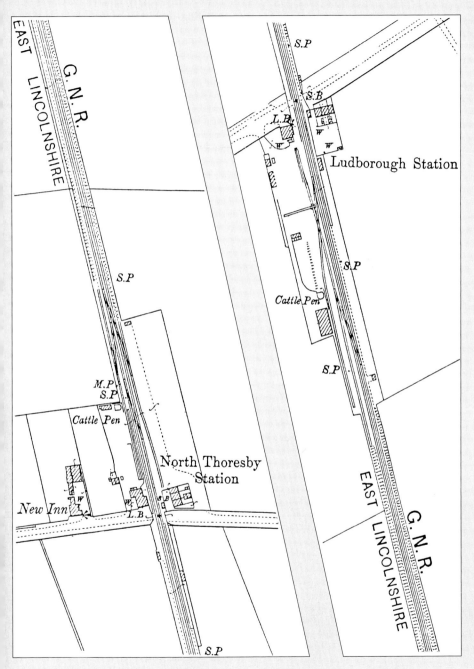

Both maps are reproduced from the 1928, 25″ Ordnance Survey maps.

An excellent period photo of a pick-up goods shunting at North Thoresby station. Engine No. 217 was one of the last 206 series Stirling 2−4−0 passenger engines. Built in 1886 it was withdrawn in 1921. *Author's Collection*

LNER steam railcar at North Thoresby. The external coal bunker on the forward-end of the vehicle indicates that this was one of the eleven supplied to the LNER after 1927, built by Clayton Wagons Ltd. of Lincoln. No. 2122 *Railway* was like the others named after former horse drawn mail coaches. Seating 64 people they were cheap to operate. This one worked from Grimsby for a short time prior to being transferred to Annersley in July 1929. *J. Hickling*

North Thoresby station looking south showing the siding behind the platform.   *D. Thompson*

Diesel locomotive, class '31', No. 113 at Holton-le-Clay station on 25th April, 1979. By this time the line had been singled and was goods only.   *M. Roughley*

Holton village halt consisting of two low rail-motor platforms with the steps used by passengers propped up against the halt buildings.   *D. Thompson*

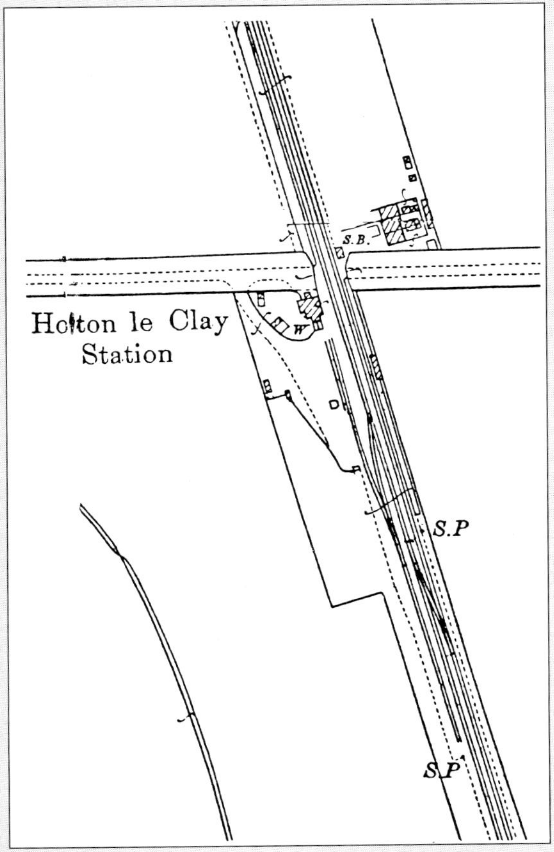

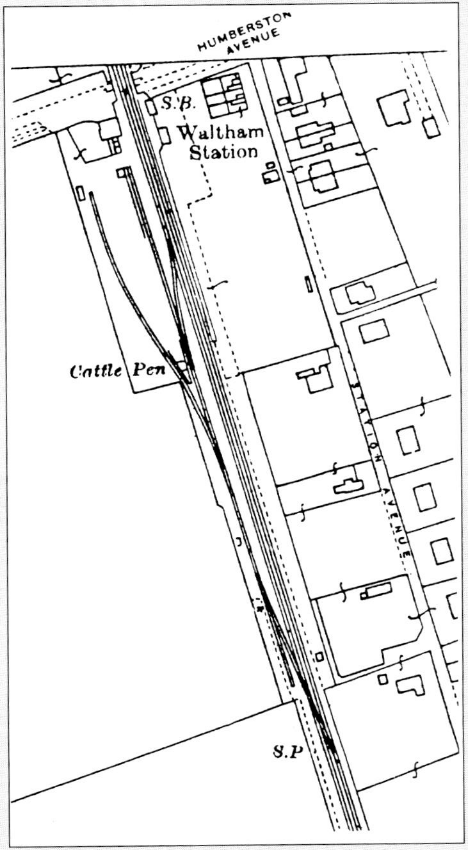

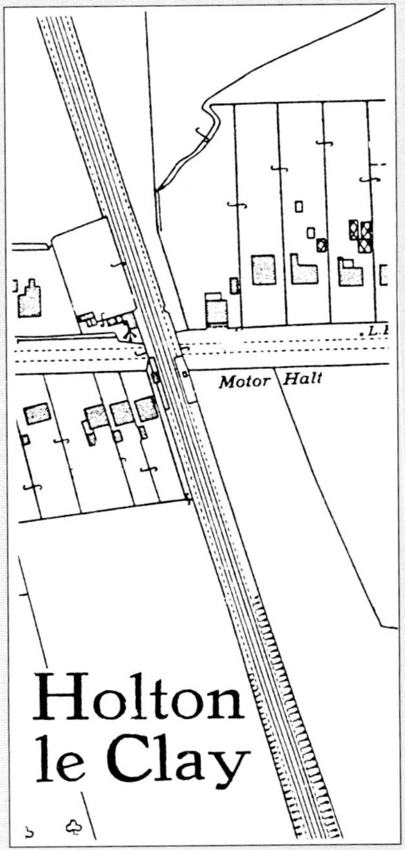

Holton
le Clay

Motor Hall

L.

S.B.

HUMBERSTON
AVENUE

Waltham
Station

S.B.

STATION AVENUE

S.P

Cattle Pen

Holton le Clay
Station

S.B.

S.P

S.P.

All reproduced from the 25", Ordnance Survey map.

The Grimsby to Louth service entering Waltham station on 10th May, 1952 with ex-GNR engine, LNER class 'C12', No. 67352 in charge hauling the former Bourne and Essendine coaches.   *M. Black*

A 1957 view of Waltham station signal box.   *H. B. Priestley*

The low railmotor platforms, waiting shelter and signal box at Hainton Street in 1961. The signal box survived until 1991 when it was set on fire by vandals and destroyed. *B. Clark*

Weelsby Road Halt in Grimsby. The level crossing was replaced by a subway in 1936. The halt served until its final closure in March 1952. *Author's Collection*

Legbourne village was adjacent to the line on the east side, the rails crossed two level crossings. Legbourne Road station was sited at the crossing furthest from the village, possibly because it was the more important of the two roads crossed. Called 'Legbourne' when originally opened, it became 'Legbourne Road', in May 1880. Passenger traffic finished on 7th December, 1953; goods continued until the station's complete closure on 15th June, 1964.

After Louth station were Fotherby and Utterby halts. Fotherby opened as 'Fotherby Gate House', on 1st February, 1852 with a service limited to market days. It closed on 28th June, 1872, and reopened as 'Fotherby Halt', on 11th December, 1905 (so too Utterby), to coincide with the introduction of the 'motor train' service. Both closed on 11th September, 1961.

Ludborough, five miles from Louth had a small yard and goods shed on the west side. Platforms were staggered either side of the road crossing which was controlled by a signal box on the east side. Ludborough offered the most comprehensive facilities on this section, the goods shed being a fine example of a type based upon the warehouse built by the Louth Navigation, at Austen Fen. The station closed to passengers on 11th September, 1961 and to goods on 25th May, 1964.

North Thoresby was similar in platform arrangement but had no goods shed; it closed to goods on 20th December, 1963, the passenger service being retained until the line's closure on 5th October, 1970.

Grainsby Halt served a Victorian hall situated two miles to the west across the A16, Grimsby to Louth road. The hall, reputed to be haunted, stood empty for many years before being demolished. The halt boasted a single storey signal cabin and opened on 11th December, 1905, was closed in 1939, but reopened after the war, finally closing permanently on 10th March, 1952.

Holton le Clay was sited south of its village on the Tetney road. Originally called, 'Holton le Clay and Tetney', the station had staggered platforms either side of the level crossing, and a signal box on the north side of the crossing. It closed to passengers in 1955.

Holton Village Halt opened on 11th December, 1905 and closed 11th September, 1961. The halt was actually in the village of Holton le Clay.

Waltham had staggered platforms either side of a level crossing and a signal box to the south of the crossing on the up side. Originally named 'Waltham for Humberstone', it was situated about 2 miles from both Waltham and Humberstone. Passenger closure was on 11th September, 1961, goods ending on 15th June, 1964.

There were two halts in Grimsby, one at Weelsby Road which opened in December 1905 and remained open until January 1940, although a subway was constructed in 1935–36, taking the road under the line. Reopened for a time after the war it was finally closed in March 1952. Hainton Street too opened on 11th December, 1905 and closed on 11th September, 1961.

Many of the intermediate stations along the ELR were sited away from the centres of population whose name they bore, the places themselves often being little more than hamlets set amongst vast areas of agricultural land. Correspondingly the amount of passenger traffic dealt with by these stations was small. George Bullock, who was signalman at Aby from 1939 until closure, said that if there were 10 people waiting for the train to Louth market they were having a good day. In contrast the 'motor train' traffic between Louth and Grimsby indicated a healthy traffic in passengers between the two centres.

Freight was an important factor in the development of the ELR and its decline a crucial consideration when closure was looming, although such decline as there was was largely down to the railway imposing controls that did nothing but alienate local business. Cattle had always been important business in Louth, where the market dated back to the reign of Edward VI. Dealers came from as far afield as Nottingham, Birmingham and Manchester, and the railway soon took its share of the traffic with stock worked in and out of the town on early passenger trains; later 30-wagon specials brought Irish cattle to market. Friday was the main day of activity with the loading docks busy between 11 am and 6 pm on that day.

The most important freight activity on the line however concerned the movement of fish, potatoes and sugar beet. The next Chapter shows how the arrival of the railway transformed the fortunes of Grimsby's fishing industry, and a similar transformation happened to the humble potato. In the early days, prior to the arrival of the ELR, they could be a difficult crop to deal with, having to be moved from the fields during the autumn and winter months when the weather could create very difficult conditions. The poor state of the roads and the bulkiness of the crop made it difficult to transport to market. The GNR was responsible for opening up the market to the Lincolnshire growers, offering generous allowances to cover the cost of cartage to the nearest railway station. Given such encouragement the potato industry rapidly expanded; harvesting began in July and between the wars traffic reached such proportions that the six or seven scheduled daily trains were increased by two or threefold.

For six months of the year between two and four hundred wagons were despatched daily from Lincolnshire to destinations countrywide, and to Hull, Liverpool, London and Southampton docks for export. Seed potatoes from Scotland were a major import into the county. Also at this time sugar beet became an important source of traffic to the railway, being moved from most wayside stations to the nearest sugar beet factory for processing. Between the wars Sibsey was dealing with up to 80 wagons of potatoes or sugar beet a day. A train left Skegness at 3.30 pm picking up wagons of potatoes (or beet in the season) at Havenhouse, Wainfleet and Thorpe Culvert, and on arriving at Sibsey the wagons were marshalled with others already there and despatched at 4.45 pm to Boston. Engines used on this duty were usually a class 'K2' or 'J6' which came in from Boston with a brakevan. During the 1920s there were two night time potato trains, from Sibsey to Bradford and from Boston to Ardsley.

Problems with this traffic began to appear as early as 1933 when the railway introduced a system of control which was in conflict with the interests of the growers. The problem was a requirement to know in advance the number of wagons needed and the precise times for delivery and collection. This was difficult for the farmers who were at the mercy of the weather and could not always predict when they would be able to get on to the land to load up. Following a meeting in the Wainfleet area in 1933, the farmers began to use road transport.

George Bullock recalled that during his time at Aby the chief freight traffic was in potatoes, sugar beet, hay, straw, cattle, 'and the odd racehorse, £20 for a round trip in a horsebox'. Aby was also sending out a ton of watercress a week and after World War II became a depot for Kelloggs, a box van coming in every three weeks for Butlin's holiday camp at Skegness. Lime was also sent from Aby, before, and during, the war but this was not a prolific trade. During the war over 45,000 tons of concrete and hardcore were delivered through Aby for the construction of Strubby aerodrome. Also during World War Two, the line was host to an armoured train consisting of a tank engine, a spare tender, two open wagons and two armoured trucks with six pounder guns. The train was also equipped with anti-tank guns, machine guns and small arms and crewed by 30 soldiers. These type of units operated along the east and southern coasts as support to the Army in the event of invasion. On one occasion the train was required at Spalding but had to be split at Aby in order to make way for a scheduled train. According to George Bullock the manoeuvre involved, 'a lot of shoving about', to get the armoured train into the sidings. Based at Louth in July 1940, the following September it was at Grimsby with visits to the Mablethorpe loop and Skegness and it moved to Spalding in 1941 before being based at Boston, from where it continued to patrol the ELR.

During the bad winter of 1947 the line was reduced to single line working because of snow; meat was sent out from the larger centres of population such as Louth or Alford to the smaller stations from where it was delivered to the villages by station staff on Saturday mornings. February 1947 was described as the black and white month, too little coal and too much snow, with frost unparalleled in the country's history. One hundred passengers, including the Grimsby Town football team returning from a game at Chelsea, found themselves stranded at Louth, the local caterer being called from his bed in the early hours to provide much-needed refreshment. During the same month 150 passengers, some of whom had been 19 hours on a train, were given hospitality by the station master at North Thoreseby, in his own and the station staff's houses.

There were many crossings along the ELR, and accidents and mishaps no doubt occurred at all of them during the lifetime of the railway. Ings Lane, near Little Steeping signal box, certainly had its share, the earliest occurring in November 1897. Tom Odlin was killed by a train whilst crossing the line with two horses pulling a wagon of corn. It was late harvest time and a foggy day, which no doubt helped to deaden the sound of the engine, the wagon being pushed down the line for some distance. Mrs Parrinder, the wife of the gatekeeper at Mill Lane, Little Steeping, had that day gone to Boston by train. Whilst waiting on Boston station for the train home she, and the other waiting passengers, were hustled into a waiting room and told to remain there as there had been a bad accident at Little Steeping. Naturally Mrs Parrinder was concerned for the welfare of her husband and most relieved to find him safe upon her eventual return.

There were two crossings at Little Steeping distinguished by the descriptions Long Crossing and Short Crossing. Locals said that if there was a train standing in Little Steeping station there was not enough time to cross the line.

In 1946 Ted Dales, who farmed the land close by the Short Crossing, had contractors cutting cabbages for him. A load was being taken across the line by lorry, five men were in the cab with Ted sitting on the back. He saw the train coming and jumped clear, but the train caught the rear of the lorry scattering cabbages everywhere, fortunately no one was hurt. The last reported accident at Little Steeping involved Mr Bray and his farm trailer which was hit by a dmu at Ings Lane crossing at about 7.15 in the evening. Thirteen passengers were transferred to another train travelling in the opposite direction; no one was injured but the damaged unit remained at Little Steeping overnight and was moved the next morning.

Pasture Street crossings, Grimsby, c.1955. Class 'K1' No. 62019 rounds the curve from Garden Street Junction with a train for Cleethorpes. The line running past the goods shed on the left was the link between the East Lincolnshire line at Goods Junction and the docks. Virtually every structure seen behind the signal box has now been demolished.   J. McCulloch

Chapter Nine
The Port of Grimsby

The development of Grimsby can be traced back to its mention in the Domesday Book in 1086, 'Having a church with a priest, a mill worth four shillings yearly and a ferry worth five shillings per annum.' The Grimsby Haven, a small river running into the River Humber, was the first harbour and around this the town grew. In 1201 King John granted the town its first Royal Charter. For several centuries the harbour remained of comparatively little importance until the Grimsby Haven Company was formed in 1796. The company obtained Parliamentary powers to, 'widen, deepen and generally improve the Haven.' The result of this was the first enclosed dock with a water area of 6 hectares, opened in 1801. This was to become known as the Old Dock and was later incorporated into the Alexandra Dock.

Realising the geographical significance of Grimsby and its great potential as a port the MS & LR extended its services to the area, and, in 1846, purchased the Grimsby Haven Company. Under the authority of the Grimsby Dock Act of 1849, the latter constructed the Royal Dock, which was opened by Queen Victoria in 1852. The Union Dock was constructed to link the Royal and Alexandra Docks and the Alexandra was extended to its eventual size. The first of three specialist fish docks was opened in 1856, Number 3 fish dock opening in 1934. A feature of the Royal Dock, and an important local landmark, is the hydraulic water tower at the dock entrance, built in the style of the Palazzo Publico, in Sienna. The tower 94.2 metres in height was built to provide hydraulic power for the lock gates and other equipment. In a book published in 1929, entitled *Port Facilities in Great Britain*, Grimsby is described thus: 'The port is an important centre for fishing in addition to which a considerable quantity of coal, machinery, general merchandise etc. are exported and timber, foodstuffs, ore, woodpulp and general cargo imported.'

Between 1871 and 1880 the contractors Logan and Hemingway were involved in much work in the Grimsby area. This included repairs to and extensions to the walls of the Royal Dock; the new fish dock lock and extensions to the fish dock pontoon, a graving dock and a further fish dock; also a connecting Cut between the Royal Dock and the Old Dock, and, finally, the West Marsh Dock. All this work came under the charge of James Hemingway, until his death in 1879.

In the latter stages of the work, Charles Hemingway came to the site; he has left a first hand account of the conditions at Grimsby.

In October (1878), I went to join my father on the works at Grimsby. I was there till May 1880, during which time we engaged on the following: completion of the walls in the Royal Dock, the connecting Cut, the new West Marsh Dock, and a quay wall to the Old Dock with piled corners to the entrance to the West Marsh Dock, also the Haycroft Drain diversion, so I had a busy time and learned a lot of valuable information which I found most useful in later life. The ground at Grimsby was very bad to work. It was 80 feet down before we got a solid foundation, alluvial deposit all the way. We excavated trenches 40 feet deep and then drove piles over the bottom 40 feet long. On this were placed capsills of whole-timbers, 14 × 14 inches and then 6 inch planking on top of that. On this the Dock wall is built, with

A superb aerial history of Grimsby is captured in these two pictures. The Royal and Union docks are on the left and the fish docks on the right. The Grimsby–Cleethorpes railway line enters alongside Grimsby engine shed at the bottom right (*opposite*), passes Grimsby Docks station, the dock offices and curves off to the right through the fish docks.

E. Green

an ashlar face and rubble backing. The trenches were timbered with whole-timber sheeting at the sides and ends; the stretchers and walings were also of whole timbers, and even then it was only just strong enough in the connecting Cut to keep the trench open. So soft was the muck that the bottom used to squeeze up with the outside pressure and the men had to stand on planks to clear away the muck as it rose whilst the capsills and planking were put on the pile-heads. I have never seen anything so bad since. My father knew how to handle the job, and he had a splendid staff of experienced men, timbermen, pile-drivers, navvies and masons, led by Israel Collins (Whistler Dick, the men called him), who was one of the finest gangers I ever came across. I also met Mr Charles Sacré, the Chief Engineer for the new works, also Locomotive Engineer for the MS&LR. He was a bluff, hearty individual with a good practical mind for the work, but I think he shone more as a locomotive engineer.

An article in the *Railway Magazine* in 1902 described the Grimsby Fish Traffic.

It is as a fishing port, of course that Grimsby ranks supreme, being indeed, the first in the world. About half of the town's 63,000 population is said to be dependent on the fishing industry and the fishing fleet which numbers between 500 and 600 vessels and gives employment to some 5,000 hands.

The quays all along one side of the two docks are covered over the whole of their width, and the side next to the water, save for frequent gaps, is boarded in. A lengthy shed is thus formed, of which the land side is left open; here numerous rails are laid, which enable the fish trains to be drawn up alongside, the level of the roadway being sufficiently below that of the 'fish pontoon', as the whole length of the market quays is known, as to bring the floors of the trucks flush with the flags of the pontoon. On these flags the fish is sold and bought, so that it will be seen that a distance of only a few feet have to be traversed in transferring the scaly spoil from trawler to train.

One by one the trawlers steam slowly up to No. 1 Dock, squeeze through the narrow gateway and take their position in the long line of similar vessels that are moored; stem on, to the pontoon quay. The operation of unloading the fish depends upon the nature of the cargo. If the vessel has come off a lengthy voyage with salted fish, the latter will be hauled out of the baskets, and forthwith wheeled into the market and laid out for inspection. But if the fish is still living and is intended for sale as fresh killed fish it has first to be despatched with a mallet before it can be unloaded. The luckless creatures are hauled up in a long handled net, pitched on the deck, in a struggling flapping mass and are promptly knocked on the head by two or three brawny hands. The fish killed, a couple of hands are employed in transfering the catch to the pontoon where it is arranged in neat rows according to size, the finest fish being placed in the front rank.

By eight o'clock or soon after, the business of unloading completed, the market presents a remarkable sight with its serried rows upon rows of fish. Then the buying begins. The approach of the auctioneer is announced by the clangorous clamour of a loud bell, vehemently rung by the gentleman himself, he continues the deafening din until a small knot of buyers gathers around him. Then his oration begins. The fish are sold by numbers, the finest specimens by fives or tens, the smaller by rows. With a clap of the hands a row of fish is sold and the group moves on to another and the proceedure is repeated. The ceaseless patter of the auctioneer and the mysterious manner in which bids are made – for not one of the buyers appears to utter a word, or even wink an eye – make the scene a most entertaining one to watch. Meanwhile the successful buyer, after appending his initials to the auctioneer's book, tears in two a narrow slip of paper bearing his

runs off at the bottom right, the line to the docks and Cleethorpes runs in the opposite direction.
Reproduced from the Second Edition, 25" Ordnance Survey map

A fine view of Grimsby Town station showing the level crossings at each end of the station. A goods train passes platform three while a 'J94' shunts carriages. In the station a train waits to depart along the East Lincolnshire line seen curving off to the right just beyond Garden Street crossing at the top of the picture.   *E. Green*

firm's name, and places the halves upon the two endmost fish of the row just purchased. The fate of the fish is soon apparent. Whilst the buying has been going on, a number of porters, with large tubs on trollies, have been busily collecting the fish purchased by their own firm.

Next comes the cleaning and packing and the loading on to the train. A few trains wait a short distance from the fish docks necessitating the consignments of fish being taken there by light carts. But the great majority of the fish trains are shunted alongside the pontoon with the result that packing is rapidly accomplished. The rolling stock used is of two kinds: salt fish and that which can be packed in boxes, barrels or crates, is carried in latticed vans similar to those used for the meat, fruit or milk traffic; while fresh killed fish is conveyed in special fish trucks. These contain three deep compartments, or tanks, in which the fish is packed between plentiful layers of ice. As soon as they are loaded up the fish trains proceed through the docks to Grimsby Docks Station and thence out on to the main lines.

The traffic in fish increases year by year and the development of Grimsby can scarcely be better illustrated than by a comparison of the figures for 1854, at the opening of the era of the port's prosperity, and for 1900. In the first mentioned year 453 tons of fish were sent away; in 1900 the total reached 133,791 tons.

Grimsby Town station comprised substantial, practical rather than ornate, buildings served by two platforms with a bay at the eastern end of platform 1, which served the Louth motor trains and was later used for parcel traffic. The station was built with an overall roof and three tracks laid through the station, the centre line being used for carriage storage. By the turn of the century a third platform had been added creating, with platform two, an island platform. Avoiding lines used by goods and excursion traffic were laid around the outside of platform 3. It became practice for down Great Central Railway trains, to Cleethorpes, to use platform 1, up trains from the same company to use platform 3, and occasionally platform 2. Trains for GNR lines used platform 2 for both up and down services. The station lay between two level crossings, Garden Street and Wellowgate, this effectively restricted the station to an overall length of 288 yards. The result was that several trains a day, notably the Cleethorpes–Kings Cross service, would block one of the crossings whilst standing at the station.

A locomotive depot was built to the south-east of Grimsby Docks station. Its importance diminished with the opening of Immingham shed, in 1912, and was in later years used primarily for servicing the large fleet of shunting engines used within the dock area. Just south of the shed were coaling facilities and a turntable, originally moved from Louth, although this had disappeared by early in the 20th century. There are a lot of gaps concerning the history of Grimsby depot particularly the role it may have played with regard to the Louth–Grimsby workings. The GNR certainly maintained a small staff of enginemen at Grimsby; from the 1920 and 1924 WTTs it is clear that the last train from Louth to Grimsby remained at Grimsby overnight. It is possible that the 5.50 am to Louth each morning was worked by Grimsby men who may have returned home with the 6.42 am goods from Louth. In the evening a second set could have taken the 7.35 pm goods from Grimsby to Louth and returned on the 9.28 pm passenger train. More information about these workings is required.

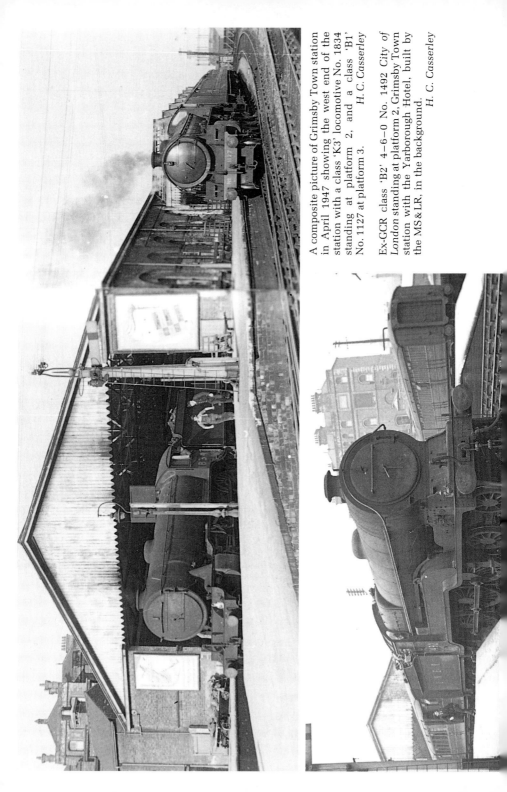

A composite picture of Grimsby Town station in April 1947 showing the west end of the station with a class 'K3' locomotive No. 1834 standing at platform 2, and a class 'B1' No. 1127 at platform 3.   *H. C. Casserley*

Ex-GCR class 'B2' 4–6–0 No. 1492 *City of London* standing at platform 2, Grimsby Town station with the Yarborough Hotel, built by the MS&LR, in the background.

H. C. Casserley

Chapter Ten
Timetables and Operation

Prior to the opening of the GNR's London terminus, at Kings Cross, on 7th August, 1850, connections with London beyond Peterborough were via either the Eastern Counties with their terminus at Bishopgate Street, or the London and North Western to Euston Square.

The Great Northern and East Lincolnshire Railway timetable for 1st March, 1849, advertised six up weekday trains between New Holland and Boston, beginning with the 7.10 am from New Holland, arriving at Boston at 10.15 am; this train connected with the 9.00 am from Lincoln (arriving at Boston at the same time as the New Holland train) which arrived at Peterborough at 10.20 am and at London, Bishopgate Street, at 4.20 pm.

Next was the 8.45 am mail train from New Holland arriving at Boston at 11.44 am and terminating at Peterborough at 1.00 pm. Both these trains stopped at all stations between New Holland and Boston.

The 11.00 am express from New Holland arrived at Boston at 1.05 pm calling also at Ulceby, Grimsby, North Thoresby, Louth, Alford, Burgh and Firsby. This train left Boston at 1.10 and arrived at Bishopgate Street at 6.25 pm.

The 1.30 pm ex-New Holland called at all stations to Boston with the exception of Waltham and Humberstone, Ludborough, Legbourne and Claythorpe. It arrived at Boston at 4.10 pm and Euston Square at 9.50 pm.

The 4.00 pm from New Holland called at all stations, arriving at Boston at 6.52 pm and terminating at Peterborough at 11.55 pm.

Last train of the day left New Holland at 7.30 pm, arriving at Boston at 10.34, and at Peterborough at 11.55 pm. This was a mail train and arrived at Euston Square, at 4.45 am.

Down trains over the East Lincolnshire began with the 7.15 am Louth to New Holland, arriving at 8.30. Next was the 6.20 am from Peterborough, arriving at Boston at 7.35 and New Holland at 10.30 am. The first train from London departed Bishopgate Street at 6.00 am, arriving at Peterborough at 12.15 pm, Boston at 1.40, and New Holland at 4.30 pm.

The first train stopped at all stations Louth to New Holland, and the latter two stopped at all stations between Boston and New Holland.

The 10.30 am express left Euston Square arriving at Boston, via Peterborough, at 3.50 pm. Stops beyond Boston were as for the up express, arrival at New Holland was at 6.07 pm.

The 11.30 am from Bishopgate Street left Peterborough at 4.15 pm arriving at Boston 5.40, then calling at all stations and arriving at New Holland at 8.15 pm. The latter part of the journey was by Parliamentary train, which left Grimsby at 7.40 pm.

Last train of the day was the 8.40 pm mail train from Bishopgate Street, arriving at Peterborough at 1.15 am, Boston at 2.51 and New Holland at 5.36 am. This train stopped at Firsby, Burgh, to unload mail and newspapers for Skegness, Alford with mail and newspapers for Mablethorpe and Sutton-on-Sea, Louth with mail and newspapers and Grimsby, parcel mail only, Great Cotes and Ulceby.

There were three up and three down trains on Sundays, up trains leaving New Holland at 8.45 am, 4.00 and 7.00 pm, arriving at Boston at 11.48 am, 7.22 and 10.34 pm respectively. The first two stopped at all stations to Boston, the first arriving at Bishopgate Street at 9.40 pm, the second terminating at Peterborough at 8.50 pm. The third was a mail train stopping at all stations to Louth, then Alford, Burgh, Firsby and Sibsey; arrival at Euston Square was at 4.45 am.

Down trains left Peterborough at 8.00 am and Bishopgate Street at 7.00 am and 8.40 pm, arriving at Boston at 9.15 am, 5.15 pm and 2.51 am and New Holland at 12.10 pm, 8.05 pm and 5.36 am respectively. The first two stopped at all stations between Boston and New Holland; the latter was a mail train.

Fares from London to Grimsby were 35s. first and 27s. second class by express, 31s. 6d. first, 24s. second and 14s. third class, by ordinary service. First and second class market and day tickets were issued to Boston from stations on the ELR between Alford and Boston, entitling the holders to travel by ordinary or express trains. Day tickets, were available on Tuesdays and Fridays between Grimsby and New Holland only on third class trains at 2s. each. Passengers were instructed to have their ticket re-stamped at the return station for it to be recognised as a day ticket. Carriages and horses could be conveyed to and from all first class stations, grooms travelling with the horses in their care being charged third class fare. The timetable also sternly proclaimed, 'No gratuity under any circumstances is permitted to be taken by any servant of the company.'

THE PONTOONS, GRIMSBY   93867

Lumpers unloading fish from a trawler ready for the early morning fish auctions. The fish would be graded and laid out according to size.   *Author's Collection*

APPENDIX

TO THE

BOOK OF RULES AND REGULATIONS

AND TO THE

WORKING TIME TABLES.

For information of officers and servants of Company only.

JUNE 1ST, 1912,

AND UNTIL FURTHER NOTICE.

EAST LINCOLNSHIRE LINE.

Absolute.

Distance from King's Cross passenger station.								
107	24½	Boston station	..	..	..	..		Boston.
107	40½	Grand sluice box	..	16	..	..	See loop line	
107	41	„ „ crossing (No. 118) ¶	..	0½	..	..		
107	61½	East Lincoln junction and box ..	..	20½	..	..		
107	69½	Tattershall road crossing (No. 1) •	..	8	..	..	.. ..	
108	4	Robin Hood's walk „ („ 2)	..	14¼	..	..	.. ..	
108	27	Redcap lane crossing („ 4)	..	23	..	..	.. ..	
108	65½	Maud Foster box .. .. ‡	..	38½	..	..	Sundays 4.0 a.m. to 10.15 a.m., 4.15 p.m. Sundays to 6.0 a.m. Mondays	
108	66	Horncastle road crsng. (No. 7) ¶	..	0½	..	..	.. ..	
108	69¾	Maud Foster drain crsng. („ 8) •	..	3¾	..	..	.. ..	Sibsey.
108	76½	Pilley's lane crossing („ 9) •	..	6½	..	..	.. ..	
109	28¾	Cross cut lane „ („ 10) ..	..	32¼	..	..	.. ..	
110	15¼	Wells „ „ („ 13) •	..	66½	..	..	.. ..	
110	35¼	Hurn road „ („ 14) ..	..	20	..	..	.. ..	
110	53	„ „ „ („ 15) ..	..	17¾	..	..	.. ..	
111	4¾	High Ferry „ („ 16) ..	..	31¾	..	..	.. ..	
111	23	„ box .. („ 17) ‡	..	18¼	..	..	Sundays 6.0 a.m. to 9.0 a.m.; 9.0 p.m. Sundays to 6.0 a.m. Mondays	
111	23½	Boston and Spilsby road crossing ¶	..	0½	..	..	.. ..	
112	5	Sibsey station	..	61½	..	..	.. ..	
112	7¼	„ box	..	2¼	..	Up	Week-nights 11.0 p.m. to 5.0 a.m.; 11.0 p.m. Saturdays to 8.45 a.m. Sundays; 8.45 p.m. Sundays to 6.0 a.m. Mondays	
112	8	„ crossing .. (No. 20) ¶	..	0¾	..	..	.. ..	
112	25	Ward dyke lane crossing („ 22) •	..	17	..	..	.. ..	Old Leake.
113	57¼	Hobhole Bank crossing („ 28) ¶	1	32¼	..	..	.. ..	
113	58¼	Old Leake box	..	0¾	..	..	.. ..	
113	58¾	„ „ crossing (No. 29) ¶	..	0½	..	..	.. ..	
113	61¼	Old Leake station	..	2¾	..	..	.. ..	
114	10¾	Seminary house crossing (No. 32) •	..	29¼	..	..	.. ..	
115	17¾	Lade bank crossing („ 35) ..	1	7	..	..	.. ..	East Ville.
115	19¼	„ „ box .. .. ‡	..	1½	..		*Open during Summer months only* ..	
116	24	Boston & Spilsby rd. crsng. („ 38) •	1	4¾	..	..	.. ..	
116	76	East Ville station	..	52	Down	Up	.. ..	
116	78¼	„ „ box	..	2¼	..	..	Week-nights 10.0 p.m. to 6.0 a.m.; 10.0 p.m. Saturdays to 6.0 a.m. Mondays	
116	78½	„ „ crossing (No. 41) ¶	..	0¼	..	..	.. ..	
117	63½	Black Drove crossing („ 45) ..	..	65	..	..	.. ..	
118	54¾	Bellwater junction	..	71¼	..	..	.. ..	
118	57¼	Bellwater crossing („ 47) ..	..	2½	..	..	.. ..	
118	57½	„ „ box .. .. ‡	..	0¼	..	..	*Open during Summer months only* ..	
120	18	Little Steeping station ..	1	40½	..	..	.. ..	Little Steeping.
120	20	„ „ box	..	2	..	..	.. ..	
120	20½	„ „ crsng. (No. 52) ¶	..	0½	..	..	.. ..	
120	71	Ings lane crossing („ 54) ..	..	50½	..	..	.. ..	
121	72	Spilsby and Wainfleet Low road crossing .. .. (No. 57) ..	1	1	..	..	.. ..	
122	1¾	Firsby south junction box ..	..	9¾	..	..	Open during Summer months and on special notice only	Firsby.
122	2½	„ junction	..	0½	..	..	.. ..	
122	22½	East junction box	..	20	..	..	Week-nights after last train is clear to 5.30 a.m. after passing of last train Saturdays to 5.30 a.m. Mondays	Do.

Extract from the 1912 Appendix to Book of Rules & Regulations.

EASTERN DIVISION—EAST LINCOLNSHIRE LINE—*continued.*

Block working.	Distance from King's Cross passenger station. Miles	Chns.	Stations, sidings and signal boxes.	Distance from point to point. Miles	Chns.	Shunting sidings. Down.	Up.	Closed	Stations to which the signal boxes and sidings are attached.
Absolute.	122	22¼	Firsby east junction	..	0½	..	..	.. .. ..	Firsby.
	122	30¾	Firsby, Skegness line junction ... (Distance from south junction)	..	28½	..	..	.. ..	
	122	33	„ Spilsby line junction ..	..	2¼	..	..	.. ..	Do.
	122	34	„ station box	..	1	..	..	Sundays 4.15 a.m. to 8.30 a.m.; 8.30 p.m. Sundays to 3.30 a.m. Mondays	
	122	35	„ crossing .. (No. 59) ¶	..	1	..	..	.. ..	
	122	38¼	**Firsby Station**	..	3¼	..	..	.. ..	
	122	50½	Firsby north box .. .. †	..	12¼	..	Up	Points worked by Porters as required.	
	123	2	Irby lane crossing (No. 61) ..	..	31¼	..	..	.. ..	
	123	24¼	Bratoft „ („ 62) *	..	22¼	..	..	.. ..	
	124	35¾	**Burgh station**	1	11¼	..	..	.. ..	Burgh.
	124	38¼	„ box	..	2½	..	..	Sundays 4.30 a.m. to 8.30 a.m.; 8.30 p.m. to 6.0 a.m. Mondays	
	124	39	„ crossing .. (No. 66) ¶	..	0¾	..	..	.. ..	
	124	73¼	Orby lane crossing („ 68) ¶	..	34¼	..	..	.. ..	
	124	74	„ box .. .. .. ‡	..	0¾	..	..	Nightly 5.30 p.m. to 6.0 a.m.; 5.30 p.m. Saturdays to 6.0 a.m. Mondays	
	125	71¾	Boothby lane crossing (No. 72) ..	..	77¾	..	..	.. ..	
	126	2¾	Welton lane „ („ 73) ..	..	12	..	..	.. ..	
	127	24½	Hanby „ „ („ 78) *	1	20¾	..	..	.. ..	
	127	50½	Dawber „ „ („ 79) ..	..	26	..	..	.. ..	
	128	0	Willoughby crossing („ 81) ¶	..	29¼	..	..	.. ..	Willoughby.
	128	0¾	„ box	..	0¾	..	..	Week-nights, 12.0 midt. to 6.0 a.m.; 12.0 midt. Saturdays to 10.45 a.m. Sundays; after passing of No. 2 up to 3.45 p.m.; 5.0 p.m. to 7.45 p.m.; after passing of No. 14 up Sundays to 6.0 a.m. Mondays	
	128	3¾	**Willoughby station**	..	3	..	..	.. ..	Do.
	128	7	„ jct. of Mablethorpe br.	..	3¼	..	..	.. ..	
	128	8¾	Willoughby junction box †	..	1¾	..	..	Open only for passing of branch traffic	Do.
	129	16¼	Well Beck Wath crossing (No. 85)	1	7¼	..	..	.. ..	Alford.
	129	62	Well lane crossing („ 86)	..	45¾	..	..	.. ..	
	130	43¼	**Alford station**	..	61¼	..	..	.. ..	
	130	45½	„ box	..	2¼	Down	..	Sundays, after down Grimsby mail is out of section to 10.40 a.m.; after No. 2 up is out of section to 2.15 p.m.; after No. 15 down is out of section to 7.15 p.m.; after No. 14 up is out of section to 3.40 a.m. Mondays	
	130	46	„ crossing .. (No. 89) ¶	..	0½	..	..	.. ..	
	131	35¾	Ailby lane crossing („ 92)	..	69¾	..	..	.. ..	
	132	26	Greenfield lane crossing („ 95)	..	70¼	..	..	.. ..	
	133	52¾	Aby box	1	26¼	..	..	.. ..	Aby for Claythorpe.
	133	53¼	„ crossing .. (No. 99) ¶	..	0¾	..	..	.. ..	
	133	56½	**Aby station for Claythorpe**	..	3	..	..	.. ..	
	134	76¼	**Authorpe station** & crsg. (103) ¶	1	20	..	..	.. ..	Authorpe.
	134	76¾	„ box	..	0½	..	..	.. ..	
	135	50½	Muckton lane crossing (No. 106)	..	53¾	..	..	.. ..	Legbourne Road.
	137	13	„ Low lane crsng. („ 110)	1	42½	..	..	.. ..	
	137	40	Legbourne wood lane „ („ 111)	..	27	..	..	.. ..	
	137	55¾	Green lane crossing („ 112)	..	15¾	..	..	.. ..	
	138	0	Watery lane „ (No. 113) *	..	24¼	..	..	.. ..	
	138	34½	Legbourne road crsng. („ 114) ¶	..	34½	..	..	.. ..	
	138	34¾	**Legbourne road station & box**	..	0¼	..	..	12.0 midt. Saturdays to 9.0 a.m. Sundays, 9.0 p.m. Sundays to 4.0 a.m. Mondays	
	139	11	Manby lane crossing (No. 116) *	..	56½	..	..	.. ..	
	139	69¼	Mablethorpe junction box ..	..	58¼	.	..	Week-nights, after passing of Mablethorpe Branch last train to 10 minutes before first train for Mablethorpe is due to leave Louth; after passing of Mablethorpe Branch last train Saturday to 10 minutes before first train for Mablethorpe is due to leave Louth Mondays.	Louth.
	139	72	„ junction	..	2¾	..	..	.. ..	
	140	1	Stewton lane crossing (No. 118) *†	..	9	..	..	.. ..	Do.
	140	50½	Wragby junction	..	49¼	..	..	.. ..	
	140	51¾	„ „ box	..	1¼	..	..	Week-nights, after the last train from Bardney is out of section until 10 minutes before the first train is due to leave Louth for Bardney following morning, from the same time Saturdays to the same time Mondays	
	140	52¼	Monks Dyke lane crsng. (No. 119) ¶	..	0¾	..	..	.. ..	Do.
	140	77½	Louth south box	..	25	..	..	Week-nights, about 12.0 midnight to 4.0 a.m.; 12.0 midnight Saturdays, or after up goods is out of section to 4.0 a.m. Mons.	
	140	79½	**Louth station**	..	2	..	..	.. ..	
	141	11	Keddington Rd. crsng. (No. 120) ¶	..	11½	..	..	.. ..	
	141	12	Louth north box	..	1	..	..	Sundays 4.30 a.m., or after No. 1 down mail is out of section to 10.10 a.m.; 11.0 a.m. to 2.30 p.m.; 8.0 p.m. to 4.0 a.m. Mondays.	
	143	36¼	**Fotherby "halt"**	2	24¼	..	..	.. ..	
	143	37	Fotherby box .. .. .. / Fotherby lane crossing (No. 125) *	.	0¾	..	..	Week-nights, after passing of No. 67 up motor car or last Excursion train to 11.0 a.m. After passing of 67 up motor car or last Excursion train Saturdays to 11.0 a.m. Mondays	
	145	49	**Utterby "halt"**	2	12	..	..	.. ..	Ludborough.
	145	49¾	Pear Tree lane crossing (No. 131)	..	0¼	..	..	.. ..	
	146	26½	Ludborough box	..	56¼	..	..	Week-nights, 7.50 p.m. to 7.50 a.m.; 7.50 p.m. Saturdays to 7.50 a.m. Mondays	
	146	27	**Ludborough statn.** and crsng. (No. 133) ¶	..	0¼	..	..	.. ..	
	147	74½	**Nth. Thoresby stn.** & cg. (No. 136)	1	47¼	..	..	.. ..	North Thoresby.
	147	75	„ „ box .. ¶	..	0½	..	..	Nightly 11.0 p.m. to 6.30 a.m.; 11.0 p.m. Saturdays to 11.0 a.m. Sundays, 9.0 p.m. Sundays to 5.30 a.m. Mondays	

EASTERN DIVISION—EAST LINCOLNSHIRE LINE—*continued.*

Block working.	Distance from King's Cross passenger station. Miles	Chns.	Stations, sidings and signal boxes.	Distance from point to point. Miles	Chns.	Shunting sidings. Down.	Up.	Closed	Stations to which the signal boxes and sidings are attached.
	148	52¼	Grainsby "halt"	..	57¼	..	..	.. ..	North Thoresby
Absolute.	148	53¼	Grainsby lane crossing (No. 138)	..	0¾	..	..	.. ..	Holton-le-Clay.
	149	66¼	Holton-le-Clay statn.&csng. (No. 140)	1	13	..	..	.. ..	
	149	66½	,, box .. ¶	..	0¼	..	..	Week-nights, after out of section has been received for last up car to 8.0 a.m.; after out of section has been received for last up motor car Saturdays to 8.0 a.m. Mondays	
	150	48¼	Holton Village "halt" ..	..	61¾	..	..	.. ..	
	150	48¾	,, road crossing (No. 142)	..	0½	..	..	.. ..	
	151	71¾	Waltham box	1	23	..	..	Week-nights, 12.0 midnight to 7.0 a.m.; 12.0 midnight Saturdays to 7.0 a.m. Mondays	Waltham.
	151	72¼	,, crossing (No. 148) ¶	..	0½	..	..	.. ..	
	151	72¾	Waltham station	..	0½	..	..	.. ..	
	154	4¼	Weelsby Road "halt" ..	2	11½	..	..	.. ..	
	154	5	Weelsby road crossing (No. 152) •	..	0¾	..	..	.. ..	
	154	31¾	Hainton Street "halt" ..	..	26¾	..	..	.. ..	Grimsby goods, G.N.
	154	32¼	Hainton street box	..	0½	..	.	.. ..	
	154	32¾	Welhome road crossing (No. 153) ¶	..	0½	..	..	.. ..	
	154	44	Grimsby gas works siding ..	..	11¼	..	..	.. ..	
	154	49	,, corporation electric station siding	..	5	..	..	.. ..	
	154	49¼	,, goods junction .. .	..	0¼	..	..	.. ..	
	154	56¾	,, G.N. ,, .. box ..	..	7½	..	..	11.0 p.m. Saturdays to 4.0 a.m. Mondays	Do.
	154	72	Pasture street crossing (No. 154) •	..	15¼	..	..	.. ..	
	154	75	Grimsby G. N. goods station †	..	3	..	..	.. ..	G.C.R.
	154	75¼	,, Holme st. crossing ¶	..	0¼	..	..	.. ..	
	154	75½	,, ,, ,, box ..	..	0¼	..	..	.. ..	
	154	76	,, ,, ,, junction	..	0½	..	..	.. ..	
	154	71½	Grimsby passenger junction with G.C.R. (Distance from Grimsby goods junction)	..	22¼	..	..	.. ..	Do.
			Grimsby Town station ..						

Immingham class 'B1' 4–6–0 No. 61366 approaches Authorpe station on 11th July, 1959 with what looks like a fish van attached to the rear of the passenger train.
H. B. Priestley

Omnibuses connecting with trains included one leaving the White Hart and George Hotels in Spilsby at 8.55 am, taking passengers to the second up train and the third down train at Firsby. Another left Spilsby at 3.00 pm, taking passengers to the fifth up and down trains. An omnibus from Burgh attended all trains except the last up service. A Wainfleet omnibus left the Woolpack and Angel Inns, at 7.30 am for Firsby, taking passengers to and from the second up and down trains, and to and from the third down train. Another left Wainfleet at 1.20 pm, taking passengers to the fourth down and the fifth up trains. Omnibuses also attended the trains at Boston, Lincoln, Louth and Spalding.

In July 1858, the GNR advertised excursions to the Lincolnshire sea coast; return tickets would be issued for up to 28 days, 'until further notice', on Mondays, Thursdays and Saturdays only from the undermentioned stations to Burgh, for Skegness; Alford for Mablethorpe; and Grimsby, for Cleethorpes at the following reduced rates:

	Burgh & back		Alford & back		Grimsby & back	
	1st	2nd	1st	2nd	1st	2nd
Louth	3/6	2/9	2/6	1/9	3/6	2/6
Boston	4/–	3/–	5/–	3/3	10/–	7/6
Tattershall	6/–	4/9	7/–	5/–	12/6	10/–
Spalding	6/6	5/–	7/6	5/6	12/6	10/–
Peterborough	9/6	7/–	10/6	8/–	15/–	11/6
Grantham	15/–	11/6	16/–	12/6		
Nottingham	15/–	11/6	16/–	12/6		
Lincoln	6/6	5/–	7/6	5/6		
Horncastle	6/6	5/–	7/6	5/6		

An omnibus left Skegness to meet the up trains at Burgh arriving at 11.12 am and 6.12 pm, and returned after meeting down trains arriving Burgh at 1.07 pm and 6.39 pm. An omnibus left Alford, on Mondays, Thursdays and Saturdays, for Mablethorpe and Sutton-on-Sea on the arrival of the down train at 1.25 pm. Conveyances for Mablethorpe could also be obtained at the White Hart and Windmill Inns, Alford.

Trains over the ELR increased to a peak of 17 trains each way just prior to World War I, but eventually levelled out to 12 each way on weekdays and two on Sundays. Sunday in Lincolnshire was a pretty quiet day as far as the railways were concerned. On the ELR there was just the 10.00 am Grimsby to Peterborough, arriving there at 12.50 pm and returning from Peterborough at 2.15 pm, back into Grimsby at 5.08 pm. Until 1925 the Sunday Grimsby to Peterborough train was worked by Louth men, in that year, however, it became a duty of Immingham shed. It is possible that one Louth crew prepared and took the engine to Grimsby and worked the train back to Louth where a second crew took it to Peterborough and back. The arrangement was no doubt altered in 1925 to avoid opening Louth shed on Sundays. The 2.15 pm was double-headed as far as Boston by a Peterborough locomotive.

Goods trains consisted of the 4.50 am Boston to Grimsby, a 12.15 am Kings Cross to Grimsby, the 5.45 am Whitmoor to Grimsby, West Marsh, and

Grimsby Town and Boston.] [Great Northern.

Bradshaw's timetable for July 1922.

Boston and Grimsby Town.]   [Willoughby and Louth.

The main content of this page consists of railway timetables printed sideways (rotated 90°), showing train services for BOSTON, FIRSBY, SKEGNESS, WILLOUGHBY, LOUTH, and GRIMSBY TOWN.—Great Northern, and WILLOUGHBY, SUTTON-ON-SEA, MABLETHORPE, and LOUTH.—Great Northern.

NOTES.

A Via Grantham. On Wednesdays passengers travel via Peterboro' and Spalding.

Z Arrives Mablethorpe at 2.37 and Sutton-on-Sea 3.15 aft. on Thursdays.

¶ "Halts" at Fotherby and Utterby, between Louth and Ludborough; Grainsby, between North Thoresby and Holton-le-Clay; Holton Village, between Holton-le-Clay and Waltham; Weelsby Road and Hainton Street, between Waltham and Grimsby Town.

e Stops when required to set down on informing the Guard at the preceding stopping station.
c Stops to set down from London.
d Saturdays only.
s Saturdays only.
f Through Carriage to Grimsby Town.
† Arrives 8 minutes later on Sats.

Through Train, Lincoln to Skegness, see pages 358 and 359.

Through Express, Nottingham (Vic.) to Skegness, Sutton-on-Sea, and Mablethorpe, see pages 367 and 360. — **Fridays only.**

Through Express, Nottingham (Vic.) to Skegness, Sutton-on-Sea, and Mablethorpe, see pages 366 and 360. — **Saturdays only.**

Wednesdays only.   Except Wednesdays.

Through Express, Derby to Skegness, see pages 366 and 360.

Through Express, Leicester (dep. 9.25 mrn.), see pages 361 and 360, and Nottingham (Vic.), see pages 366 and 360, to Sutton-on-Sea and Mablethorpe. — **Saturdays only.**

Through Express, Leicester to Skegness, see pages 361 and 360. — **Saturdays only.**

Through Express, Nottingham (Vic.) to Skegness, see pages 366 and 360.

Through Express, Nottingham (Vic.) to Skegness, Sutton-on-Sea, and Mablethorpe, see pages 366 and 360. — Except Saturdays.

Through Express from Lincoln, see pages 358 and 359.

WILLOUGHBY, SUTTON-ON-SEA, MABLETHORPE, and LOUTH.—Great Northern.

Through Express from Nottingham (Vic.), see pages 367 and 360.— **Fris. only.**

Through Express from Nottingham (Vic.), see pages 366 and 360.— **Sats. only.** Except Sats.

Through Express from Nottingham (Vic.), see pages 366 and 362, and Leicester, see pages 361 and 360. **Sats. only.**

Through Express from Nottingham (Vic.), see pages 366 and 360. Except Saturdays.

Except Fridays.

Fridays only.

the 9.40 am Kings Cross to New Clee, fish empties. In the opposite direction there was the 5.50 am West Marsh to Whitemoor, the 8.40 am worked the same route; the 9.45 am Grimsby to Boston, the 1.45 pm (FX) and the 2.35 pm (FO) Grimsby to Boston. Then came the number one express fish train leaving Grimsby Docks for Kings Cross at 6.08 pm, followed by the number two express fish for the same destination leaving at 7.15 pm, and finally the 7.35 pm Grimsby to Boston goods.

Before 1923 there had been great rivalry between the GNR and the Great Central Railway (formerly the MS&LR) over the transport of fish from Grimsby Docks. The GCR had always maintained a dominant position and at the time of the 1923 Grouping was despatching eight complete fish trains a day, plus a considerable number of fish vans attached to the rear of passenger trains. In addition to London, fish trains headed for Liverpool, Manchester, the Midlands and the West Country, mostly fully braked and run at passenger train speeds. Great emphasis was placed upon punctual and prompt delivery of this highly perishable traffic. Trains were supposed to be restricted to 45 wagons but this was often exceeded, indeed, I have been told of trains of between 60 and 100 short wheelbase wagons roaring through stations with scant regard for their blanket 60 mph speed restriction.

These heavy trains were worked by the powerful GCR 4-6-0 'B7' class locomotives, which had succeeded the class 'B5s'. From 1928 the LNER-designed 0-6-0 class 'J39s' were used and, in 1930, the powerful ex-GNR 2-6-0 class 'K3s'. The first of this class, No. 1000, when allocated to New England shed worked this duty. (The 'K3s' were replaced by 'Britannias' in about 1961, the latter also replaced 'B1s' on the morning Grimsby to Kings Cross passenger train and the 4.00 pm Kings Cross to Cleethorpes return working.) In the 1924 rationalization plans the London fish traffic was diverted over the ELR because it was quicker and less congested than the old GCR route. Under this new arrangement the working of the London fish was transferred from the GCR men to the former GNR shed at New England (Peterborough).

In 1925 Peterborough had two weekday workings to Grimsby and return for which duties large 'Atlantics' were used. The first engine stood pilot at Peterborough North from midnight until departing at 3.10 am with the East Lincs Mail, which reached Grimsby at 5.20 am. The train went on to New Holland at 5.50, arriving at 7.12 am. The return working left New Holland at 8.30 am, Grimsby departure was at 9.15 with the through Cleethorpes to Kings Cross express which reached Peterborough at 11.22 am, giving a total mileage of 194 and about four hours 'mileage pay' to the enginemen. The other locomotive took the 6.45 am 'all stations' to Grimsby, arriving at 9.50 am, returning on the 12.20 pm semi-fast, which reached Peterborough at 2.33 pm. Later a second set of men worked the engine to Boston, leaving Peterborough at 5.50 pm with the through Kings Cross to Cleethorpes express. This arrived at Boston at 6.33 pm and the locomotive remained there until 9.37 pm when it took over the 8.10 pm from Grimsby which reached Peterborough at 10.23 pm. On Saturdays the return working was the midnight goods which terminated at Peterborough at 2.20 am.

There were two fast goods trains each weekday between Peterborough and Grimsby. The first left Peterborough at 5.05 am (12.12 am from Kings Cross), and the second at 1.15 pm (9.40 am No. 1 express fish empties from Kings Cross). In GNR days both these duties were undertaken by Gresley two-cylinder 2–6–0 class 'K2', although from 1921 the new 3 cylinder 2–6–0 class 'K3' took over the latter duty. The engine from the early morning duty remained at Grimsby until it worked the 7.15 pm No. 1 express fish to Kings Cross, due at New England at 9.55 pm. The second engine worked the first fish train from Grimsby at 6.00 pm, reaching Peterborough at 8.26 pm. After working to London the engine from this train worked the 12.12 am down goods.

A 2–8–0 ran light from New England, Saturdays excepted, to Boston where it turned before continuing to Old Leake, which it left at 4.30 pm with the Class 'A' vegetable train to Kings Cross, arriving there at 4.20 am after changing crews at Peterborough.

Jim Storr was a fireman at Boston in the 1950s and had a good knowledge of East Lincolnshire workings to and from Kings Cross:

> Boston men worked to Kings Cross some years before the 'Britannias', appeared. There were two drivers who had the necessary road knowledge and they worked excursions to and from the capital before 1939, as well as during the Second World War and the late 1940s. The first regular turns were introduced about 1950, with Boston men working one of the evening fish trains, ex-New Clee, returning with the class 'D' (goods), which left Kings Cross after midnight, also the morning express from Cleethorpes to Kings Cross and the 4.00 pm return. An interesting summer only roster gave Boston men the 1.00 am Kings Cross–Newcastle/Edinburgh, as far as Peterborough, a heavy train loading up to 14 vehicles on some days and, of course, Pacific-powered. On Fridays only, the 12.30 pm, Grimsby to Peterborough was extended to Kings Cross and we double-headed the train from Boston to Peterborough. After taking water, we drew forward to release the train engine and then coupled up to the train again to work forward to Kings Cross. Both engine and men lodged overnight (the 'BI' at Top Shed, the crew at Kentish Town Hostel), in order to work back the 8.00 am Kings Cross to Skegness on Saturday morning. There was also an 8.05 am to Skegness but New England provided the 'BI' for that train. On the return journey we were relieved by another Boston crew at Boston, who worked the 'Butlins Express', forward to Skegness and then back to Kings Cross with the lunch time express ex-Skegness.
>
> On summer Saturdays in the 1950s we were also required to work the two morning expresses, around the 9 o'clock mark, from Skegness to Kings Cross as well as the Saturday morning extra from Grimsby Docks. I am certain that the 'BI' off the latter returned double-heading the 4.00 pm down, however, there was, at one time, a Cleethorpes express on Saturdays leaving London at about 2.18 pm and I recall this being double-headed on several occasions. I also remember some Sundays when the morning train from Cleethorpes to Kings Cross was strengthened to 15 vehicles and we used to run light engine to Firsby to couple and assist through to London, returning with the down train in the evening. My heaviest load unassisted was a night parcels train consisting of 14 bogie vans and 12 empty passenger vehicles – heavy work for the 'BI' and the fireman.

In the summer of 1951, between 18th June and 23rd September, East

Lincolnshire trains working to and from the capital were as follows:

Up

9.00 am	SO	Skegness–Kings Cross (arr. 11.55 am) 7th July to 8th September.
9.15 am	SO	Skegness–Kings Cross (arr. 12.22 pm).
8.07 am	SO	Grimsby Docks–Kings Cross (arr. 12.42 pm) 7th July to 8th September.
8.57 am	EWD	Cleethorpes–Kings Cross (arr. 1.13 pm MFSX, 1.20 pm MFSO).
12.25 pm	SO	Skegness–Kings Cross (arr. 3.35 pm).
12.30 pm	FO	Grimsby–Kings Cross (arr. 4.40 pm).
3.04 pm	EWD	Grimsby–Kings Cross (arr. 10.05 pm FSX, 10.07 pm FSO).
6.15 pm	SO	Skegness–Kings Cross (arr. 9.32 pm) until 8th September.
8.50 am	SUN	Cleethorpes–Kings Cross (arr. 2.30 pm).
5.50 pm	SUN	Grimsby–Kings Cross (arr. 9.50 pm).

Down

8.00 am	SO	Kings Cross–Skegness (arr. 11.00 am) until 1st September.
8.05 am	SO	Kings Cross–Skegness (arr. 11.07 am) until 15th September.
10.55 am	SO	Kings Cross–Skegness (arr. 1.55 pm) until 8th September.
4.00 pm	EWD	Kings Cross–Cleethorpes (arr. 7.54 pm).
2.40 am	SUN	Kings Cross–Boston (arr. 6.33 am) Newspapers.
6.18 pm	SUN	Kings Cross–Cleethorpes (arr. 10.53 pm).

Of these trains, the 3.04 pm ex-Grimsby was not advertised as a through train in the public time table. This was not surprising as it formed the 7.05 pm 'slow' from Peterborough and London-bound passengers could linger at the North station for the express at 8.09 pm and still be in Kings Cross some 20 minutes earlier. The Saturdays only extra from Grimsby Docks at 8.07 am was unusual in that it ran via the Mablethorpe loop. The up Sunday morning service, notwithstanding its scheduled 12 bogies, made 21 intermediate calls between Cleethorpes and Peterborough and ran with class 'B' headcode to that point, taking all but 10 minutes of 4 hours. The buffet car must have been very welcome. The Sunday Kings Cross to Boston newspaper train included a Third corridor in its formation, (subsequently used for the afternoon train to Doncaster via Woodhall Junction and Lincoln) but was not advertised. In addition, the stock of the 6.55 am express from Grimsby to Peterborough (arr. 9.01 am), formed the 9.22 stopping train from Peterborough to Kings Cross but this was advertised neither in the Working nor the Public books, presumably as it would be necessary to shunt at Peterborough North to allow passage of the 7.35 am Nottingham Victoria to Kings Cross.

One set worked each weekday on the 8.57 am up and the 4.00 pm down. Curiously, a different set worked the Sunday 8.50 am up and the 6.18 pm return, and stood spare on weekdays; intensive stock utilization was a thing of the future. The 9.00 am and 12.25 pm (8th to 22nd September only) ex-Skegness, and the 8.07 am ex-Grimsby Docks, all 12 vehicle trains, had no return workings. However, the 9.15 am ex-Skegness was reduced by one Composite Corridor and formed the 8.00 pm Kings Cross to Doncaster on Sundays. The 12.30 pm (FO) from Grimsby attached three Third Corridors at Peterborough and then worked (until 1st September) the 8.00 am (SO) Kings Cross to Skegness, which in turn formed the 12.25 pm back to London. The

8.05 am down on Saturdays turned round to form the 12.40 pm Skegness to Derby Friargate, whilst the 10.55 am down became the 6.15 pm return ex-Skegness. The 3.04 pm and the 5.50 pm (Sun) were basically 5 vehicle sets comprising, Twin Brake Third/Third Corridor, Composite Corridor, Twin Third/Brake Third Corridor, which also worked the majority of the East Lincolnshire trains between Peterborough and Grimsby and covered stopping services to and from Kings Cross as part of their circuits. Of course, attaching and detaching took place at various points to cater for peak loading, for example, the 5.50 pm up from Grimsby on Sunday evenings had six Third Corridors added to complete its formation.

The second advertised, 'all year' through service did not commence until the summer of 1954. The 6.55 am from Grimsby was altered to run non-stop from Peterborough in advance of the 7.35 am ex-Nottingham and returned at 6.18 pm from Kings Cross, but advertised through to Cleethorpes. It is interesting to note that the stock of this service and that of the 8.57 am (9.20 am SO) and the 4.00 pm (4.15 pm SO) return, worked the Sunday through trains alternately.

During the summer from 1956 to 1962, the second up morning Cleethorpes train was diagrammed for a quick turnround in London instead of returning in its Mondays to Fridays path at about 4.15 pm. Departure times from Kings Cross were at 2.08 pm in 1956 and 1957, 2.18 pm from 1958 to 1961 and 2.15 pm in 1962. However, this break with tradition was carried even further between 1956 and 1959 by diverting the train at Firsby South to run to Skegness, reverse and regain the main line at Firsby station.

An ex-GCR class 'C4' No. 2906 crossing Garden Street crossing and entering Grimsby Town station from the East Lincolnshire line on 16th April, 1947. No. 2906 still carries the abbreviated wartime 'NE' on its tender side.   *H. C. Casserley*

The freight timetable commencing in October, 1946, was as follows:

Up
am

3.30	'C' Mineral	Frodingham–Whitemoor
4.45	'C' Mineral	Grimsby–Whitemoor
6.30	Cattle	Louth–Willoughby (FO) Q (Q = Run as required)
7.20	'B' Goods	Grimsby GN–Boston
8.30	'C' Mineral	Frodingham–Whitemoor

pm

1.45	'A' Goods	Grimsby GN–Boston
5.27	No. 1 Fish	Grimsby Docks–March
6.02	No. 1 Fish	Grimsby Docks–Kings Cross
7.03	No. 1 Fish	Grimsby Docks–Kings Cross
8.45	'B' Goods	Grimsby GN–New England

Sunday

| 5.00 pm | LE | Grimsby, West Marsh–Boston |

Down
am

12.40	No. 2 Fish Exp.	Kings Cross–Grimsby GN (MX)
1.15	'C' Mineral	Colwick–Immingham (MX)
3.35	'C' Mineral	Colwick–Immingham (MO)
5.45	'A' Goods	Boston–Grimsby, West Marsh
5.50	No. 2 Exp. Goods	Whitemoor–New Clee
7.00	'A' Empties	Whitemoor–Grimsby, West Marsh
8.00	'B' Goods	Boston–Grimsby, West Marsh
9.55	No. 1 Fish Empties	Kings Cross–New Clee
10.21	'A' Empties	Whitemoor–Frodingham
11.20	'C' Mineral	Colwick–Immingham

pm

1.00	'B' Goods	Boston–Louth
1.30	No. 2 Veg.	Algarkirk–Newcastle
2.30	No. 2 Veg.	Algarkirk–Newcastle
3.00	No. 2 Veg.	New England–Grimsby, West Marsh
3.00	'A' Goods	Whitemoor–Grimsby, West Marsh

Sunday

| 2.20 pm | 'A' Goods | Boston–Grimsby, West Marsh |

The last steam-hauled service train to run from Cleethorpes to Kings Cross was hauled by 'Britannia' 4–6–2 *Clive of India*, which ran with a headboard declaring, 'The last steam hauled train, Cleethorpes–Kings Cross', on 4th November, 1962. The train left Grimsby at 5.35 pm and was No. 70040's last regular working on passenger trains. After they ceased to work passenger trains the Immingham 'Britannias' were used on the Grimsby fish trains over the ELR. The very last steam engine to haul a passenger train from Cleethorpes to Kings Cross was No. 4472, *Flying Scotsman*, on 21st October, 1967. In July 1969 No. 4472 worked a train over the East Lincolnshire but did not call anywhere to pick up.

Dick Dunnett, a young fireman based at Immingham towards the end of World War II, described a firing trip over the ELR:

We would book on duty at Grimsby Loco. at the required time, have a look at the notice board and make our way to Grimsby Town station, where our engine would be waiting. Perhaps a 'Lord Farringdon' four-cylindered ex-GCR express engine, with a load of 14 well filled coaches. Quite a lot of our passengers would be servicemen, particularly on a Friday when many of them would be going home on 24 or 48 hour weekend passes.

We would take over from an Immingham crew who had worked the engine down from the main depot. If they had done the job right they would have given the firebox a good plastering of coal and topped-up the tender with more coal before leaving Immingham. I would at once set about my job, check that the smokebox door was tightly closed, the front plate was clear of smokebox char as this could nearly blind you once you got moving fast. Check that the head lamps were correctly placed and lit if required, that the water tank was full, the coal safely stacked and the fire irons safely racked. On the footplate I would examine the brick arch to make sure it was complete, the tubeplate clean, and the gauge glasses clean and registering correctly. Next, give the firebox a good round to be burning through. Crack up as much coal as possible into fist sized pieces, sweep and slack down the footplate, then I checked the injectors. By now it would be time to watch for the guard's signal to start the train, relayed by the station staff.

The boiler would be three parts full and the steam pressure would be nearly lifting the safety valves. As we pulled round the very sharp right hand curve towards Grimsby Town signal box, I would watch the passage of our train out of the station until it was on the straight and we were passing Hainton Street signal box. I would now start firing and would go round the box with ten or twelve shovelfuls according to the size of the coal I had managed to crack up earlier; slack coal was always directed into the back corners of the firebox. On with the exhaust injector as the boiler level would now be down to half a glass, this injector would be left on for most of the journey. Hopefully by now the safety valves would be simmering and the fire shaping into best steaming condition. The driver had no need to watch me, he could judge the effectiveness of my efforts by watching the smoke effects at the chimney which would tell him if he had the steam pressure required to work his train.

We would be now in sight of Waltham distant signal and if it showed clear another ten or twelve shovelfuls would go round the box and on with the other live steam injector as the engine was being worked very hard to get some speed into the train. From Waltham the Holton bank was in our favour allowing the driver to pull her up a couple of notches and we could now recover an inch or two of water. We would be now passing Holton-le-Clay and as soon as North Thoresby distant signal was seen to be clear another round of coal went into the box and on with the live steam injector. The slightly favourable gradient helped to gain the permitted line speed. A level stretch before the climb through Ludborough, off with the injector and another round of coal, this time a little heavier because of the gradient. Through the road bridge beyond Fotherby and the Louth distant would be straight ahead. On with the injector, the line cleared left and then straightened out into the station, the falling gradient into the station having been taken care of by earlier braking. Off with the injector, get the right away from the guard and watch the train out of Louth station. Fire up, through the road bridge, the line now bearing right past Mablethorpe junction and now a regular pattern of firing and feeding the boiler as we passed Aby and Authorpe. Alford station roof had been in sight some miles away; the approach was on a falling gradient. A pull up here to platform the rear coaches and then back to the old routine past Willoughby, Burgh-le-Marsh and on to Firsby.

From Firsby the line was level and dead straight until the approaches to Boston. Passing Little Steeping, Bellwater Junction, Eastville, Old Leake and Sibsey, most of these sections were about the same in length and distant signals were easily spotted. Firing was regular to maintain steam pressure at maximum and water level in the boiler in the top of the gauge glass. The approach to Boston was over two very severe curves that were taken at 15 mph, first left, then right, then straight down the gradient to the water column at the south end of the platform. Off with the injectors while filling the tank, a quick flash around the box with the jet on hard to lessen the smoke emission. Wait for the guards 'right away'; often at Boston it was necessary to pull up the train to position the rear coaches at the platform.

Working days were conditioned by many factors, not least by your driver and his handling of the engine. The reversing gear, if a screw gear, would usually mean he would use the steam provided by the fireman more economically, the reason being that it was not as hard to pull up on the rack and the expansive properties of high pressure could be used to best advantage. With a lever reverser which often required considerable effort to notch up, the practice was often to pull it up to about 30 per cent cut-off and leave it there, the regulator opening being used to tune the train, not the most economical use of fuel and water.

The pattern and frequency of firing was determined by the shape and size of the firebox, this could vary between 27 sq. ft on a 'Lord Farringdon' type Belpaire box, 31 ft on a GNR Atlantic to 41 sq. ft on a 'Green Arrow', the largest type of my early firing days.

The size and quality of the coal provided varied from huge lumps down to house fire sized nuts, slack and briquettes, these latter being a size from $12 \times 9 \times 9$ inches to ovoids. Very few two days were the same, loads differed day to day, the same engine two days running could give you a good day or a bad day. The shape of the firebed was very important, and required considerable skill to maintain it in the best steaming condition, particularly with some of the indifferent quality fuel provided.

With a stopping train the stopping and starting created havoc with your fire, necessitating a deeper firebed to prevent the blast lifting live coals out of the chimney, when blasting away from each station to reach line speed as soon as possible. It was necessary to fire round the box when leaving each station, the amount of fuel patterned round depending on the length of section and the weight of the train. The drill was to watch the train out of the station, fire round the box, injector on; as soon as the valves simmered or, on a short section when the distant signal was sighted, off with the injector as you ran into the station (unless the safety valves had lifted) to allow pressure to build up for a quick getaway. With over 40 stations between Grimsby and Peterborough and back with a heavy train of usually nine coaches the tender would be stripped and the firebed a mess in spite of a good clean at the turn round point; you certainly went home tired.

Chapter Eleven
Louth to Grimsby workings

The services between Louth and New Holland were worked by both MS&LR and GNR trains. A timetable of 1st April, 1848, shows that there were five trains a day each way on weekdays and two each way on Sundays. Only one weekday train each way and one Sunday train each way carried first, second and third class passengers, the others were restricted to first and second classes. The three class trains were always the first trains of the day. Fares were, first class 2d. a mile, second class, 1½d. a mile and third class, 1d. a mile. From February 1853, one up and one down train called at Fotherby gatehouse on the two market days each week, this later became Fridays only until 1872, when the trains ceased stopping at Fotherby.

The inauguration of the 'motor train' service between Louth and Grimsby on 11th December, 1905 saw the opening of several halts along the line, at Hainton Street and Weelsby Road in Grimsby, Holton Village, Grainsby, Utterby and the re-opening of Fotherby. The halts had short, low platforms, the railmotors having steps for passenger use at such places. The decision to use railmotors on the section between the two towns was taken in October 1905. The decision was no doubt based upon several factors, the distance between the two towns was not too great, the line was straight and reasonably level. Railmotors could not carry much water and could not cope with heavy gradients.

The service was operated by steam railcars comprising a small locomotive attached to a saloon coach. The locomotive section consisted of an orthodox 0–4–0T having outside cylinders 10 in. × 16 in. and 3 ft 8 in. wheels. The coach part was finished in the standard teak of GNR carriage stock, the locomotive portion was green. These railcars were capable of being driven from either end thus enabling a quick turnround at the end of each trip and consequently a more frequent service. The railcars provided eight return trips on weekdays, the service being augmented on Wednesdays and Saturdays by an ordinary steam train in each direction. The rail motor worked through from Grimsby as far as Sutton-on-Sea on the Louth, Mablethorpe and Willoughby loop. The services on the Louth–Grimsby section began at 6.00 am and continued at intervals until 11.00 pm, the journey taking 45 minutes. Passenger trade built up so much that on busy days the railmotor could not cope with the demand. Sometimes on market days and Saturdays an extra coach would be attached, and the units also pulled the occasional horse box or box van.

The use of railmotors was a response by the GNR to the increase in motorised road traffic and its economical consequences. A 32 seater Daimler petrol-engined railmotor was tried out on the Hertford line in 1905 but proved too unreliable for use in service.

The GNR Board opted for steam-powered railmotors, and six were ordered in April 1905, two from Avonside numbered 7 and 8 and costing £2,440 each. At first fitted with side tanks, by the time No. 8 was photographed at Louth around 1906 the tanks were no longer in evidence. Numbers 5 and 6 came from Kitsons at a cost of £2,400 each, the carriage sections being manufactured by the Birmingham Carriage and Wagon Company. Numbers

1 and 2 were designed by Ivatt and built at Doncaster works at a cost of £2,153 each. Number 2 was given a Gresley elliptical-roofed coach. The carriages offered both first and second class and seated about 55 people. The late Albert Ogle remembered travelling regularly from Waltham to his timber business in Grimsby, 'first class but a rough old ride.'

The Louth–Grimsby service was usually worked by Nos. 5 and 6. When a railmotor service began over the Louth, Mablethorpe and Willoughby section in February 1906, No. 2 appears to have been the principal motive power, although photographic evidence shows No. 5 on the coastal loop, and No. 8 at Louth.

Nos. 1, 2, 5, 6, 7, 8, were still in service at the 1923 Grouping; two cars (numbers unknown) were withdrawn in 1925 and the remaining four in the following year. Eventually engines were separated from coaches and the coaches formed into articulated pairs; the most famous local set worked on the Horncastle branch until the 1950s.

Various experiments took place on the line including, in 1928, the use by the LNER of one of the modern steam railcars manufactured by the Clayton Waggon Company of Lincoln. The Clayton Geared Steam Rail-cars began to appear in 1927. In the 20 years that had elapsed between the early experiments with steam cars and the introduction of the Clayton vehicles, there had been little development, but soon after the Grouping the modern form of high speed geared engine with a high pressure water-tube boiler became popular. Apart from the modern motive power, the Clayton railcars were not unlike the old GNR railmotors in principle, one end comprising a passenger coach resting on a four wheel-coupled power unit having 3 ft wheels and being driven through gears by two cylinders 6¾ in. × 10 in. The superheated water tube boiler had a pressure of 275 lb. per square inch and a distinctive feature of these cars was the coal bunker outside the coach at the leading end of the power bogie. The majority had seating for 64 passengers. They were named after stage coaches. One called *Chevy Chase* was given extended trials locally, and this included trips between North Thoresby and Grimsby. The whole class was extinct by January 1937.

In 1952 a former Great Western Railway diesel railcar was given trials locally. This experiment was more successful and led to the widespread introduction of diesel vehicles in Lincolnshire. The first three came to Louth in 1955 and by 1956 all local services had been converted to diesel traction.

After the railmotors finished, the Louth–Grimsby workings were taken over by class 'D2', 'D3' or 'C12' locomotives and a 'Quad Art' set which was fitted with tip-up steps to accommodate the low platforms at the halts. A ticket rack was also provided to enable the guard to issue tickets to passengers joining the train at the halts. When the diesel multiple units took over the service moveable steps had to be provided at the halts.

In 1924 the Louth–Grimsby railmotors left at 7.05, 7.45 and 9.53 am, 12.20, 2.02 (WX), 3.00 (WO) and 5.20 pm. Return journeys from Grimsby to Louth ran at 8.40 and 11.15 am, 1.05, 2.10 (this went to Willoughby via Louth and Mablethorpe) 4.00, 5.40, 6.30 and 10.00 (ThSX), 10.30 (ThSO) pm.

The service between the two towns remained pretty much the same until 4th December, 1939 when, owing to the War, the halts at Hainton Street and Weelsby Road in Grimsby were closed. Hainton Street, however, was re-opened on 1st March, 1940. The 11th September, 1961 saw the end of the railmotor service accompanied by the closure of Hainton Street, Holton Village, Utterby, Fotherby, Waltham and Ludborough. Nine years later, on 5th October, 1970 North Thoresby and Louth closed to passengers.

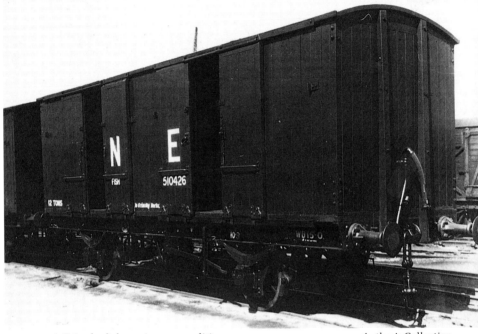

A Grimsby fish van in new condition.   *Author's Collection*

Standard class '9F' 2−10−0 No. 92193 takes the spur round to the East Lincolnshire line at Holme Street, Grimsby, with a Saturday fish train in April 1961.
Author's Collection

Chapter Twelve
Motive power

GNR DAYS

The very first two Sharp Singles, GNR Nos. 1 and 2 were delivered to the ELR to enable the contractors, Waring and Sons, to complete the ballasting between Louth and Grimsby. The GNR asked that the first two engines should be delivered to Grimsby. No. 1 was despatched from Sharp Brothers' Atlas Works in Manchester, on 3rd August, and No. 2 followed on 9th August, 1847; both were at work by the 13th at a hire fee of £2 per day. The task of ballasting took longer than anticipated and with questions of capital depreciation arising the ELR agreed to purchase the engines on 1st March, 1848. The arrangement was purely financial and after the opening of the ELR in October the GNR 'bought' them back at a valuation of £4,136 plus £92 2s. delivery costs.

Conversion of the majority of Sharp Singles into tank engines took place in 1852 at Boston works. The 2−2−2 tanks worked semi-fast trains along the ELR before settling down to a long career on country branch lines. Withdrawals began towards the end of the 1860s and the remaining 2−2−2Ts finished their days on the level East Lincolnshire lines.

The 'Small Hawthorn' 2−2−2 singles began life working passenger trains between Louth and Grimsby, and Boston and Peterborough. Some of these engines were rebuilt in the early 1860s and used on lighter secondary expresses, others worked out their time on branches. Those expecting rebuilding were all withdrawn by 1872. Nos. 67 and 70 were rebuilt by Stirling as 0−4−2s. No. 70 was noted at work in Lincolnshire attached to a Stirling 4-wheeled tender. In the early 1890s both engines were shedded at Wainfleet.

The Hawthorn 0−4−2 goods engines often deputised for the 0−4−2 Sharp rebuilds up until 1890, but took over from the Sharps on local passenger services after this date. No. 101A worked the Louth−Mablethorpe branch in charge of driver Cheeseman for many years. No. 110A had an all-over cab and served Skegness in the 1890s. Both these engines had tender weatherboards to protect the enginemen from the weather when working tender first.

No. 100 was a singular 2−4−0 engine delivered to Boston on 23rd April, 1849. Built as a prototype passenger locomotive for the opening of the GNR main line, it was the only engine designed during Edward Bury's short tenure of the post of locomotive engineer. The concept of the engine was behind the times and the prototype remained the only one to be built. No. 100 was rebuilt by both Sturrock and Stirling, and is reported to have worked satisfactorily on its duties on heavy stopping passenger trains and the easier express workings. Towards the end of the 1880s it was working around the Boston and Lincoln areas. Reboilered in 1891 it spent its last years in Lincolnshire.

'Large Hawthorn' 2−2−2 Singles were top link engines which helped the GNR to fulfill its promise to shorten the journey time between London and York. The GNR's reputation for fast running was established by these en-

Sharp 2−2−2 No. 8, in original condition seen here at Grantham in 1854. The first engines to run on the East Lincolnshire line were of this type.
Kenneth Leech

One of the original engines used on the Louth−New Holland section, No. 1, rebuilt as a 2−2−2T as seen here in 1864. *Kenneth Leech*

Hawthorn 0−4−2 goods engine No. A101 seen here at Alford. The engine was delivered to Boston on 17th February, 1848 and worked between Louth and Mablethorpe in the charge of driver Cheeseman for many years. It was withdrawn in 1897.
Alan Turner

gines but as loads increased they were relegated to secondary express work. Stirling rebuilt ten of the class and these continued on secondary passenger and stopping train duties in the mid-1880s. Nos. 204/8/9/13/4 finished their lives on the level run between Peterborough and Grimsby, No. 214 being the last of class, withdrawn in 1892.

Patrick Stirling's class 'E' 2−4−0 passenger engines proved themselves useful on a wide variety of duties, and between 1867 and 1895 no less than 139 were built. As was the policy with other classes, once the 2−4−0s began to be replaced by newer types of engines those remaining were relegated to branch line work and other secondary duties. Many found themselves in Lincolnshire, at Boston and Lincoln. Most of the Lincoln engines were sub-shedded at Louth, working trains to Grimsby, Mablethorpe and Willoughby. No. 1000A was a favourite here and in its last days was kept going for only three turns a week. Of the 34 remaining class 'EIs' in January 1923, Nos. 753/5/8,855,994/5/8/9,1061/4/8 were at Boston, and Nos. 814/67/83/7,1000A,1062/3/7/9 were at Lincoln. After 1923, a heavy withdrawal programme soon reduced the number of the class to two, No. 4070, at Lincoln, and No. 3814 at Louth; the latter was the last survivor, finally withdrawn in November 1927.

Stirling class 'F' 0−4−2 tender engines were designed to handle mixed traffic, ranging from heavy excursions to fast goods trains. By 1912 these too had a healthy presence in Lincolnshire which was maintained until 1921. Light duties abounded in the county, exemplified by No. 958, one of the last survivors, shedded at Louth and sub-shedded at Mablethorpe. Its day's work began at 8.00 am taking empty coaches to Sutton-on-Sea to form the 8.35 am passenger train to Louth, followed by a trip to Sutton, back to Mablethorpe and then to Louth again. Next a goods was worked through from Louth to Willoughby, before a final trip with the 4.45 pm passenger train to Mablethorpe. All remaining 0−4−2s were withdrawn by the end of 1921.

Stirling's beautiful 8 ft Singles successfully coped with trains of 200 tons at speeds of 54 mph and were the GNR's standard express passenger locomotive for over 20 years. By 1909 they were becoming a rare sight in London, although they did appear occasionally from Peterborough on a 'vacuum goods' Grimsby fish train. No. 1008, a Lincoln Single, was sub-shedded at Louth where it was condemned on 5th June, 1914. Nos. 1003/4, Peterborough engines throughout their careers, finished up working over the lines to Boston, Grimsby and Lincoln.

LNER AND BRITISH RAILWAYS

Before World War II, Ivatt 4−4−0s class 'D2' and 'D3' dominated the passenger traffic in Lincolnshire for many years. Shed allocations of the classes give a good indication of the consistent distribution of these types in the area.

Class 'D2'	late 1920s	1933	1939	1946
Boston	10	8	10	4
Lincoln	6	7	3	—
Louth	1	3	2	—
Colwick	12	13	8	13

GNR class 'B5' a 7 ft 2–2–2, No. 4. This locomotive was shedded at Boston in November 1905 and withdrawn in June 1906.   *Kenneth Leech*

8 ft single No. 1003 at Boston on 14th April, 1914. A Peterborough-based engine throughout its career, it was one of the last to be withdrawn on 6th May, 1915.   *Kenneth Leech*

Railmotor No. 2 built by the GNR at Doncaster and supplied with a Gresley elliptical-roofed coach. This unit worked out of Louth during the early days of the motor train service.
                    Author's Collection

Class 'D3'	1935	1939	1945	1948
Boston	8	4	—	—
Lincoln	3	4	—	—
Louth	4	1	1	1
Colwick	11	7	—	6
Immingham	1	11	11	2

As was often the case with passenger engines, some of the 'D2s' and 'D3s' spent many years at the same shed. Class 'D2' No. 4395 was at Boston from 1920 to 1947 and No. 4384 was there from 1924 to 1946. Class 'D3' No. 4359 was there for 20 years, while Nos. 4358 and 4360 were at Boston from 1912 until withdrawn in 1937 and 1935 respectively. The Boston 'D2s' worked trains to Skegness, Louth and Doncaster with trips to Mablethorpe in the summer only. Colwick 4–4–0s were used on trains to Skegness and Mablethorpe during the summer months, the engines used on these trains usually being outshedded at Leicester (Belgrave Road) and working to the Lincolnshire coast via Barkston, Sleaford and Boston.

Louth's 'D2s' performed regularly on the shed's most important weekday job, the 6.24 am, calling at most stations to Peterborough. Arriving at 8.47 am the loco worked to Peterborough East and back before taking the 10.50 Peterborough to Grimsby, where it arrived at 1.47 pm; crews changed at Louth. The engine worked the 5.10 pm Grimsby to Boston, arriving at 6.56, and finally the 8.42 pm back to Louth arriving there at 9.35 pm. Class 'D2s' from Grantham worked slow trains eastwards to Boston, Skegness and Mablethorpe.

Another familiar type on local and branch line duties was the class 'C12', 4–4–2 tank engines. Built to replace the Stirling classes 'G1' and 'G2' 0–4–4Ts on the London suburban services, rapidly increasing train weights soon begun to prove too much for them and, by 1920, they had been replaced by the more powerful Gresley class 'N2' 0–6–2 tanks and were then transferred to the country districts. The allocation in 1935 included three at Boston, three at Louth and one at Lincoln. By 1945 Boston had one, Louth six and Lincoln three. Louth 'C12s' included Nos. 4013 (BR No. 67352), 4506 (67364), 4525 (67379), 4528 (67381), 4530 (67383), 4531 (67384) and 4548 (67398). No. 4525 was at Louth in 1927 and still there in 1950. No. 4013 was one of the first batch of eleven 'C12s' distinguished from the rest of the class by having square-cornered tanks and bunkers. No. 4015 of the 1927/1935 allocations was one of the original batch.

The 'Standard' goods engines, classes 'J3' and 'J4' were employed throughout the GNR system on main line and local goods duties, as well as mineral trains; 'J3s' were still to be found in Boston's allocation in 1946. The class 'J6' were designed to work express goods trains and mixed-traffic. A Gresley modification of Ivatt class 'J2', they were familiar in Lincolnshire playing many roles; heavy coal trains, local goods and passengers as well as excursions to the Lincolnshire coast from Nottingham.

The Ivatt class 'C1' 4–4–2 Atlantics had three weekday turns over the ELR which, by 1935, had settled down to: 3.10 am East Lincolnshire Mail, Peterborough to Grimsby Town; 5.25 am Grimsby to New Holland; 8.29 am New

Holland to Grimsby and the 9.20 am Grimsby to Peterborough. The Atlantics worked special trains from Kings Cross to Immingham Dock in connection with cruise ships to Norway. In the early days these trains were usually worked through by Kings Cross men and engines, being conducted over the Boston to Immingham section; the men lodged and returned next day with a loaded train or empty coaching stock. In the years 1930/31 working methods changed and New England 'Cis' were used; Nos. 292, 279 and 1300 were all, at one time or another, associated with the Peterborough area and in particular with the East Lincolnshire line. Information about the work done by No. 292 is extremely scarce. Originally allocated to Doncaster it was transferred to Peterborough during World War I. On Saturday 8th August, 1925, it worked the Grimsby portion of the 4.00 pm from Kings Cross, which ran independently of the main train to Peterborough where it arrived behind Atlantic No. 4421, which was replaced by No. 3292 for the continuation to Grimsby. No. 292 rarely visited Kings Cross.

No. 3279 was transferred to New England in February 1935, and was regularly employed on the 6.45 am Peterborough to New Holland working arriving at 10.11 am and departing at 11.15 for Peterborough where it was due at 2.55 pm.

Class 'C2' 4–4–2, 'Klondykes' after 1923 worked secondary duties in all districts. From Peterborough they worked trains over the ELR, although they worked more frequently over the GCR sections in Lincolnshire.

The LNER introduced both ex-Great Central Railway and Great Eastern Railway engines into what had been exclusively GNR territory. Louth had ex-GCR class 'D7s' Nos. 5684, 5701, 5703 and 5711 shedded there during the 1930s. Ex-GCR 'D9' No. 6029 was there between 1938 and 1941 and class 'J11' No. 6008 was at Louth in 1934 while Nos. 64320 and 64328 were there when the shed closed in December 1956. Former GCR class 'N5' 69306 was another foreigner shedded at Louth during the 1950s.

Boston too had its share of former GCR engines in the form of 'N5s' Nos. 69256, 69261 and 69280 as well as class 'A5' Nos. 69808 and 69819 in its 1950 allocation.

In 1924 the considerable London fish traffic was diverted over the ELR because it was less congested and more direct than the original Great Central route. Under this arrangement the working of the London fish was transferred to the former GNR shed at New England.

At the time of the 1923 Grouping, the engines used on the heavy fish trains were the powerful 4–6–0 class 'B7' (GCR class '9Q'). Prior to the 'B7s' the fish trains had been worked by class 'B5s' and some of these continued to be used for this traffic. From 1928 the LNER-designed 0–6–0 class 'J39' was used, and later in the 1930s the ex-GNR class 'K3' 2–6–0s took over. The 'K3s' were replaced by British Railways class '7' 4–6–2 mixed traffic 'Britannias' around 1961.

Immingham shed was heavily involved in the fish traffic and received the 'Britannias' as follows: No. 70039 in November 1960, Nos. 70040/1 in December 1960, 70035 in September 1961 and 70036–38 the following month. From November 1960 the remaining 'K3s' were withdrawn as follows: No. 61866, December 1960, Nos. 61891 and 61966, July 1961, 61914, September,

GNR class 'H2', (LNER class 'K1') 2–6–0 No. 1630, the pioneer of the class at Boston after its initial trial run on 17th August, 1912.
P. W. Pilcher Collection, National Railway Museum

Class '9F', 2–10–0, No. 92194 of Immingham shed stands at the very beginning of the East Lincolnshire line at Holme Street, Grimsby, with a fish train for London, *c*.1961.
Paul King Collection

61912, October and 61877 in November 1961. The 'Britannias' also worked the morning Grimsby Town–Kings Cross and the 4.00 pm Kings Cross –Cleethorpes return working taking over this duty from the class 'B1s'. Immingham's allocation for 1950 included classes 'B1', 'K2', 'K3', 'D11', 'C4', 'O4', 'J11', 'N5', 'A5' and WD 2–8–0s; up until 1965 this was also to include 'Britannias' and class '9F' 2–10–0s, all of which were seen working the ELR.

The ex-GCR class 'C4' 'Jersey Lillies' had been top main line engines until replaced by the 'B17s' in 1936. There was a large post-war allocation at Boston and all of the 20 engines handed over to British Railways in 1948 were allocated to Lincolnshire sheds: Lincoln nine, Boston nine, and Immingham two. They were used in goods trains from Boston.

During the inter-war years prior to the arrival of the 'C4s', four or five former Great Central class 'D9s' were allocated to Immingham shed. From about 1928 one was allocated to New Holland shed and was employed on a double-shifted duty which involved visits to Retford and Cleethorpes in the morning, and a trip to Boston over the ELR in the afternoon. In 1938 an Immingham 'D9' was diagrammed to take the 7.15 am express from Grimsby to Peterborough connecting there with the 9.12 am London service. It finally returned to Grimsby as the 8.42 pm express. Immingham based 'C4s' soon took over this duty. In December 1938, 'D9' No. 6029 moved to Louth Shed where it remained for over three years.

During World War II a special dispensation allowed class 'V2' 2–6–2s to work over the ELR. They had previously been banned from the northern section of the line because of a weak bridge, No. 21, north of Fotherby Halt. The ban was reimposed in the spring of 1946 when class 'B1s' became available to work the line.

Diesel motive power on the ELR began with the arrival, in July 1956, of the Derby lightweight units, based at Immingham depot; those working Grimsby diagrams were stabled at Cleethorpes. Powered by two horizontal underslung engines the units could be coupled together into four, six or eight car sets. They were used for local traffic, and, at first, of course, for driver training. The latter involved working the unit from Grimsby to Boston via the Mablethorpe loop and returning via Alford and Louth. The lightweights were replaced by the heavier, more powerful, Metro-Cammell types, these in their turn being superseded by the Derby-built heavyweight units with two 238 hp horizontal underslung engines and capable of towing a parcel van. One particular diagram over the ELR involved taking a unit from Grimsby to Peterborough, stabling it and waiting to relieve a New England crew on the Kings Cross to Cleethorpes service. Lincoln became the maintenance depot for the units, refuelling being carried out by a fitter's mate at Cleethorpes and running repairs by a fitter sent from Immingham depot.

The Brush Type 2 diesels Nos. 5500–19, were the first to be allocated to the London area and worked there until late in their lives, at which point some turned up at Immingham. They carried the red symbol denoting that these units could only be coupled to units carrying the same symbol.

Locomotives from No. 5519 onwards, had a 12 cylinder 'V' 1365 hp power pack. These units carried a blue symbol and could be coupled to most other types used on the Cleethorpes to Kings Cross expresses. They were very much underpowered for dealing with these heavy, fast trains, and were eventually re-engined with 1460 hp English Electric engines. Although these were an improvement they still did not provide the required power for express workings. Much better were the English Electric 1750 hp units, but it was the arrival of the Brush Sulzer 2750 hp, 95 mph locomotive that proved to be the answer to all the problems of speed and power. As well as hauling the London service the Brush Sulzer 2750 hp diesels were used on the Merry-Go-Round services to Immingham coal terminal, fitted with slow speed equipment it was possible to reduce loading and unloading speeds to ½ mph.

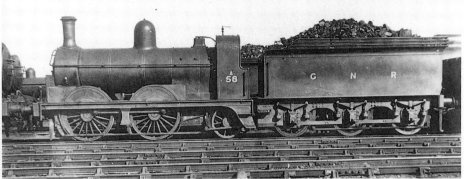

Mixed traffic 0−4−2, No. 58 as running about 1918 and shedded at Boston in 1905. From here it worked goods trains in the area.   *Kenneth Leech*

A 206 series 2−4−0 No. 1000 was a Lincoln engine sub-shedded at Louth from where it was withdrawn in 1924.   *Kenneth Leech*

Chapter Thirteen
Louth Shed

A catholic collection of locomotives, most of them elderly, was based at or worked through Louth over the years, beginning with the engines built by Sharp Brothers and Company, of Manchester, sent to inaugurate the services in 1848, then a collection of GNR engines, usually 'retired' from duties in and around London or on the main line. Finally a mixed collection of ex-GNR and GCR locomotives was based there during the final years prior to the shed's closure in December 1956, because of dieselisation.

Louth had one principal duty each weekday to Peterborough. This train departed from Louth at 6.24 am, having started from Grimsby at 5.25 am behind a Grimsby engine. Arrival at Peterborough was at 8.47 am. The return working left Peterborough at 10.50 am and was worked through to Grimsby arriving at 2.01 pm, after changing crews at Louth. The engine then took out the 4.50 pm Grimsby to Boston, arriving there at 6.48 pm, and returning at 8.10 pm, due at Louth at 9.21 pm. This locomotive had then worked 223 miles which exceeded the distance worked in a day by some larger engines stationed at main line depots; Louth booked Ivatt 4–4–0s on this turn. However, during the General Strike, what amounted to the single daily working between Grimsby and Peterborough for the duration of the crisis, was worked by either of two ex-GNR 2–4–0s still retaining their original pre-Grouping numbers of 1307 and 1314 in the charge of a Louth crew (Driver Coupland and Fireman Manning).

The Sunday Grimsby to Peterborough train was worked by Louth men until the duty was taken over by Immingham depot in 1925. This working is described elsewhere. Other Louth duties included the 10.15 am passenger train to Boston, arriving at 11.40 am, returning with a goods train at 12.30 pm (except on Wednesdays, when it departed at 2.50 pm). Most of the local trains to and from Grimsby were also covered by Louth shed.

When the Louth and Mablethorpe line opened in 1886, and the complete loop by 1888, Louth shed provided motive power for the branch. The GNR Working Timetable of 18th August, 1919 showed a basic service that differed little over the following years. The Mablethorpe-based engine commenced work at 8.00 am (FX), 7.50 am (FO), running light to Sutton-on-Sea to work the 8.35 am (FX), 8.20 am (FO) passenger train to Louth, due there at 9.09 or 8.59 am respectively. It returned to Sutton-on-Sea on the 9.53 am all-stations train, arriving back at 10.28 am. It then went light to Mablethorpe to shunt the yard there before taking the 11.45 am passenger train to Louth, arriving at 12.10 pm. On Mondays, Wednesdays and Fridays, the same engine then headed the 2.35 pm goods train hence, which was due at Willoughby at 4.50 pm. It finally returned light engine to Mablethorpe shed. On Tuesdays and Thursdays, the days work finished at Mablethorpe at 3.35 pm as the goods train terminated there. Saturdays saw the engine working light from Mablethorpe to Firsby from where it took a portion off the 2.40 pm express from Nottingham, departing Firsby at 4.37 pm and arriving at Mablethorpe at 5.09 pm. The main part of the train went on to Skegness, leaving Firsby at 4.35 pm and reaching Skegness 16 minutes later.

A Louth engine worked the 7.45 am passenger train from Louth to Willoughby (arriving at 8.38 am), the 8.55 am Willoughby to Mablethorpe (arriving at 9.15 am), the 9.35 am Mablethorpe to Willoughby (arriving at 9.56 am) and then the 10.35 am goods train from Willoughby to Louth, arriving there at 12.55 pm. Possibly the same engine then ran light to Mablethorpe to take over the 1.10 pm Willoughby to Louth passenger train from the engine that had worked it in. Other Louth engine workings were the 3.15 pm Louth to Sutton-on-Sea (arriving at 3.52 pm) and the 4.20 pm train back to Louth (arriving at 4.55 pm), the 5.35 pm Louth to Willoughby (arriving at 6.27 pm) and the 7.15 pm return service to Louth.

A Wainfleet engine left Firsby at 12.38 pm and ran light to Willoughby to work the 1.10 pm to Mablethorpe, arriving there at 1.30 pm and it returned with the 3.15 pm to Willoughby, arriving at 3.35 pm. The engine then went back to Firsby 'light' to resume duties on the Skegness branch.

On Mondays, Wednesdays and Saturdays, a through express left Nottingham at 9.55 am and divided at Firsby into Skegness and Mablethorpe sections, except on Saturdays. A Boston engine worked the Mablethorpe section, due there at 12.23 pm. That engine returned light engine to Firsby. On Saturdays the complete train ran through to Mablethorpe headed by a Colwick engine which left Mablethorpe at 2.30 pm for Nottingham.

To form the early morning train from Sutton-on-Sea to Louth and later branch services, three GNR coaches were based at Mablethorpe. They were numbered 338, 1449 and 1530. The Stirling 0−4−2 No. 958, then shedded at Mablethorpe, always faced towards Louth.

In 1919 engines working the Bardney branch were largely supplied by Lincoln; this arrangement changed in the reorganisation after the 1923 Grouping when Immingham took over the Grimsby to Boston workings from Louth, whilst Louth took over the working of the Bardney branch. The 1924 workings show departures from Louth at 7.45 and 10.00 am and 3.05 and 5.33 pm, the second and third trains being shown as through to Lincoln. A goods service started from Louth at 8.40 am (MWFO) and returned from Bardney at 1.39 pm. An additional goods service from Louth to Bardney only, left at 3.30 pm (FX) and 3.35 (FO) conveying cattle from Louth market.

Louth engine diagram 9 worked the 7.45 and 10.00 am as well as the 3.05 pm departures, returning from Bardney at 8.44 am, 11.29 am and 4.20 pm respectively. The 11.29 am train with the same engine departed from Louth for Grimsby at 12.20 pm, arriving at 12.50 and returning to Louth at 1.05 pm. Similarly the 4.20 pm departure from Bardney also worked through to Grimsby, departing from Louth at 5.30 and arriving back at 7.25 pm. This train then formed the 7.33 pm to Sutton-on-Sea where it arrived at 8.10 and left at 8.40, arriving back at Louth at 9.17 pm. The 1.25 pm Bardney to Louth service, which left Lincoln at 12.55 pm, was worked by a Lincoln engine and crew, who worked back the 3.30 or 3.35 pm goods. They finally took the 6.28 pm Bardney to Lincoln passenger train home.

The 5.33 pm was included in Louth shed's number 4 diagram and had worked several other duties to Willoughby and Grimsby during the day. An engine ran light from Louth to Bardney on Fridays to work the 3.28 pm back to Louth. The 8.40 am goods was number 6 diagram, doing no more work after returning to Louth at 5.05 pm. In the 1930s a passenger train would leave Louth for Bardney at 7.42 am arriving there at 8.30 am. This was followed at 8.05 am by a pick-up goods train which proceeded to Donnington-on-Bain where it waited for the 9.10 am from Bardney to pass through the station. It then moved on to Wragby, where it paused for the 9.50 am from Louth to pass before continuing to Bardney.

The only connection with Grimsby was the 11.40 from Bardney arriving at Louth at 12.40 pm. A train from the Mablethorpe branch would connect with the Grimsby train at the same time.

D.C. Allen recalled what it was like to be a loco spotter in Louth during the 1940s and 1950s:

My earliest memories of the local railway were about 1946/7 when the 'C12' 4−4−2 tank engines used to run along the single track, Mablethorpe branch line which ran parallel with Stewton Lane, where I then lived. These trains usually consisted of ancient LNER rolling stock of pre-war vintage with burnished teak exterior, brass fittings, and gold lettering and numbering. It may be of interest to know that at that time, the Mablethorpe branch not only joined the main line at Mablethorpe Junction signal box, but also had a line diverging southwards which intersected the main line opposite MacDonald's farm to form a triangle. Presumably this route would have been used for traffic in the event of the Sutton-on-Sea and Willoughby loop being inoperable. However, I never saw this route used and it was lifted in the early 1950s.

Other recollections of those boyhood days was of lingering on the approaches to the walled bridge at the junction of Newmarket and Wood Lane in the hopes of seeing the white plumes of smoke and steam drifting past as the 'Bardney Flyer' meandered by. These occurrences were infrequent for I believe that even in those days, there were only two goods trains a day, the passenger service having already been withdrawn. Timings on the Bardney Branch must have been distinctly leisurely as I can recall class 'J11' 0−6−0 No. 64320 pulling three trucks and a guards van appearing from under the bridge spanning the London Road and the driver stopping for several minutes to watch the game of cricket then in progress on Louth C.C's Ground.

In 1951 at the age of 10, I took up 'loco-spotting' in earnest. This resulted in many hours spent on Louth station with a well-thumbed Ian Allan 'spotters' book for the Eastern Region. The station at the time still sported its Great Northern overall roof and there was a well frequented W.H. Smith's bookstall on the down platform. I can remember quite distinctly lounging on platform trolleys surrounded by baskets of Louth Racing Clubs pigeons and reading the latest copy of Trains Illustrated. In the background was the sound of simmering steam engines in the shed, punctuated every so often with the steady tapping of the bell in the Louth South signal box as a train approached the station. The creaking and straining of the signal wires would then ensue as the signalman pulled off the distant and home 'pegs'.

On those early visits, the local Louth Shed allocation (40C) was 'D3' 4−4−0 No. 62132 built by the GNR Engineer H.A. Ivatt in 1896, two GCR 'J11' 0−6−0s 64320, 64328, and of course, the 'C12' GNR tanks, introduced in 1898. The 'C12s' were numbered, 67352, 67364, 67379, 67381, 67383, 67384, and 67398. The 'D3' remained only shortly as it disappeared in late 1951 for scrapping at Doncaster. The two 'J11s' were used on the Bardney Branch pick-up goods and the 4−4−2 tanks on local passenger services: to Mablethorpe and Willoughby to the south, and to

Grimsby in the north. The Grimsby service took a leisurely 45 minutes and a set of wooden steps was carried for passengers wishing to alight at Fotherby or Utterby Halt as there were no platforms there. The through traffic at this time consisted of Immingham-shedded 'B1s' on the Cleethorpes-Kings Cross passenger duties, ex-War Dept 2–8–0s, Robinsons 'O1s', 'O2s' and 'O4s' on the iron ore trains for Frodingham, 'K2s' and 'J6s' on mixed traffic goods from Boston Shed, and the Gresley 'K3s' on the fast fish freight trains from Grimsby Fish Docks. There were few named locomotives. Some that I did see on my vigils were 'B1s' named *Madoqua, Dibitag, Burghley, Lord Burghley, Fitzherbert Wright, A. Harold Bibby* and *Oliver Bury*.

The most frequently named visitor was 'B1' No. 61379 *Mayflower*, then shedded at Immingham. I can remember this engine pulling into Louth station late one evening looking in pristine condition with its smokebox gleaming and red buffers freshly painted. This was on the occasion of Brenda Fisher's return home after becoming the first woman to swim the English Channel. The down platform was packed solid with local wellwishers including local dignitaries.

The ultimate for me was the sudden appearance in 1952/3 of the rare 'B17' 4–6–0 No. 61653 *Huddersfield Town*. This engine belonged to the famous 'Footballer' class that encompassed pre-war First Division football teams. *Huddersfield Town* was the only one of its class I ever saw in the North Lincolnshire area. No. 61653 was a crack passenger locomotive, at that time shedded at 31A, Cambridge, and its normal duties would have been on the East Anglian mainline between Liverpool Street, London and Norwich. Judging from its appearance, smartly painted out in apple green livery, with its brass nameplate, football and team colours well polished, it would appear to have just been outshopped from Doncaster works after overhaul. This could explain its appearance at Louth; she may well have worked a 'running in' trip from Doncaster to Grimsby. After shunting its train of ballast into the sidings opposite the old Malt Kiln, she simmered for about an hour in the siding next to the cattle loading bay, near Keddington Road crossing, before returning light engine towards Grimsby.

My favourite engines, however, were those on the Bardney Goods as the crews of the 'J11s' were a friendly bunch who would allow illegal footplate rides as their engines ran-round their trains before shunting into the sidings and reversing into the Shed. The inevitable closing of the Bardney Branch had, for me, some compensation as the driver of the crane, hired to lift the track, was a lodger in our household, so I had several rides up the line with him. At times of inactivity, I used to pick wild strawberries on the embankments whilst the 'lodger driver' would take himself off to catch local game. The trips came to an abrupt end when the driver had to appear in Louth Court accused of poaching!!

The 'C12s' began to be phased out with No. 67352 being transferred to New England, Peterborough, and Nos. 67381 and 67383 being sent for scrap. Their replacements were equally ancient 'N5' 0–6–2 tanks with flower pot chimneys. Members of this class at Louth were Nos. 69261, 69269, 69305, 69306, 69309, 69322 and 69327. I, with countless other people, spent many minutes stranded at Keddington Road crossing as 'N5' tanks fussed over shunting endless wagons into the Malt Kiln yard. Just before the closure of Louth Shed in 1956, a number of the larger 'A5' 4–6–2 tank engines were loaned from Immingham Shed. One such locomotive that I can remember was No. 69812.

By 1958 I was living in London, but on occasional trips to Louth it was reassuring to see steam still alive, although it now took the shape of Riddles '9F' 2–10–0s and 'Britannia' Pacifics banished from the dieselised East Anglian main line. Heavy locomotives such as these had been barred in my heyday because of weight and clearance problems on the numberous bridges in the Boston area. The sight of a 'Britannia' with an exotic name like *Hereward the Wake, Sir Christopher Wren* or *Clive of India*, storming through Louth on Kings-Cross–Grimsby expresses was a spectacular sight. Nevertheless, the most nostalgic memory for me will be a three cylinder 'K3' approaching Monks Dyke Crossing with a late evening fast fish train. Silhouetted against the setting sun, it raced along the high embankment with billowing plumes of smoke and steam, rapid exhaust and the glow of its fire casting a surreal light around cab and tender.

I shall treasure those distant sounds of a railway at work. The impatient shriek of an engine whistle as the driver gave a reminder to the signal box after taking water at the platform end, or the mournful siren of a W.D. 'Austerity' with its connecting rods clanging as it lumbered along with its heavy goods train. There was also the rapid beat of the fast fish trains as they rattled south in quick succession for the next day's market at Billingsgate.

One could plot the course of these trains with the sudden heightening of sound as they rounded the northern curve near Brackenborough and the ensuing roar from the walls of the old Malt Kiln. This would be followed by the clatter of tons of steel hitting the points outside the station, immediately followed by the sudden muffling of sound within the station itself. There would then be a sudden rise in the staccato beat as the driver opened the regulator south of the station before the noise abruptly diminished in the cutting north of Monks Dyke Crossing.

The closure of the line in 1970 not only ended a communications artery for the whole of East Lincolnshire, but also meant the disappearance after 100 years of a way of life that will never be seen again.

At 4.40 pm on Wednesday 19th February, 1941, a bombing raid on Louth resulted in eight people losing their lives. Bill Botham was a fireman working in Louth at the time.

I can recall the events quite clearly, we had worked the 9.13 am goods from Grimsby to Whitemoor as far as Burgh-le-Marsh with No. 5989, one of our 'Pom-Poms', and changed footplates, swapping the 'J11' for a 'K3', which was another Immingham engine returning home with the 1.53 pm from Whitemoor. As we struck off for Grimsby there was no sign of anything untoward and certainly nothing to indicate what was to follow. At Louth we stopped for water and I climbed up to the tender while my mate Percy Mouncey turned on the water at platform level; it was at this point that we noticed the aeroplane in the east. We could not tell if it was 'Jerry' or not, as it flew northwards and no red alert had been given (the air raid warning system in force which meant that trains were held at signal boxes if danger from enemy aircraft threatened), neither Percy nor myself paid too much attention. But when the plane wheeled around towards Louth we began to look up and take notice, the pilot was obviously following the railway tracks into Louth station and using the railway as a guide. We were being attacked! Coming in fast and low the plane began firing at us, so without much ado I dived between the tender and the leading van as bullets were pumped into the woodwork of the leading vehicle. Next a bomb was released and if I had thought I had been lucky to dodge the bullets I was doubly fortunate to escape being blown to pieces when the missile hit the platform and bounced, without exploding, into a dead end siding where it finally went off.

After the plane had gone I scrambled down on to the platform in search of my driver, who I had last seen sheltering behind the water column. Realising we were under attack Percy had decided to stay put and by standing close to the column had escaped the bullets, but when the bomb exploded a piece of flying metal had caught his face and nearly severed the tip of his nose, not that I realised this at the time. When I saw him clutching his face his hands covered with blood, I assumed

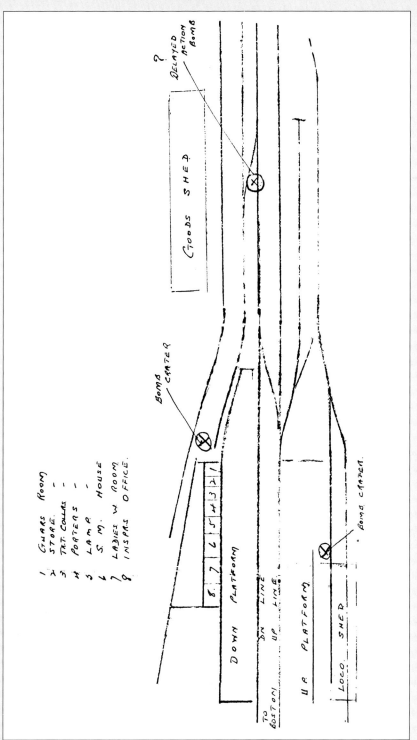

Enemy action at Louth: the Plan accompanying the Report on the next two pages.

3421)
P 3⁄4 Rms.—1-41.

The Great Northern Railway Company.

REFER HERETO
IN YOUR REPLY

STATION MASTER'S OFFICE,

LOUTH, ___ Feb 21st, 1941.___

Report of Damage etc caused by Enemy
Action at Louth. Feb 19th, 1941.

At 4.40.pm. on Wednesday Feb 19th, an enemy plane circled
over the station and town of Louth, dropped some bombs, and then
machine- gunned the town. Two H.E. Bombs fell directly on the
station and exploded, causing damage to the station buildings,
rolling stock, and some casualties,(one fatal)
It was thought that a Delayed Action bomb had fallen on the
down main line and in consequence of this working on the down line
was suspended, and all traffic worked under Single Line Regulations
over the up road.

Damage.   The Guards Room, and store room next door were practically
-------   demolished.   Considerable damage was done to the
following by broken windows and falling ceiling etc.
Goods Offices.   Ticket Collectors Room.
Porters Room.   Lamp Room.
Ladies Waiting Room. Inspectors Office.
Booking Office.   General Waiting Room.
The station house was badly damaged with broken windows
doors blown off, and a large number of slates off the roof.

The loco shed received a direct hit causing damage, and
blowing a large hole in the side wall of the station arcade.
The following stock was damaged.
Engine No 6008.   B.C.L. 43072.   C.L. 41379.
B.T. 41581.   Halt Saloon. 41344.
Double Bolster. L. N. S. 322236.
The Halt Saloon and Carriages suffered chiefly from broken
windows, the double bolster was completely wrecked.

Some damage was also done to wagons on No 80 down Whitemoor
Frodingham goods train, no record was taken of this damage.
This train at the time of the attack was stood in the station
getting water.

Some damage was discovered done to the down main line, and it
was assumed a delayed action bomb was there. This caused the
down main to be closed and all traffic was worked over the
up main line between Louth Sth and Louth Nth Signal Boxes
S. L. W. in operation between the hours of 6.10.pm and
10. 0. pm.   It was then agreed that no bomb was there.

The Great Northern Railway Company.

STATION MASTER'S OFFICE,

Sheet No 2.

LOUTH, _____ 21. 2. 41.

Coal Merchants Offices and sheds in the goods yard were also damaged, and several slates were blown off the station roof etc.
The clock in the booking office was blown off the wall, and one ticket case was blown in the floor mixing up all the tickets.
Gas and water mains were broken, temporary lighting was fixed up by means of candles and Hurricane Lanterns.

Casualties.   Fireman C. Bradley. Louth Loco. received fatal injuries.

Porter. H. S. Stanley. Louth. received cuts on the face, First Aid was rendered by the Louth Ambulance Class, and Stanley was sent to the local Hospital for treatment and detained there.
Motor Driver F. Cope. Mablethorpe. (working at Louth at the time) received cuts on the face. First Aid rendered, but the injuries were not serious and Cope travelled home that night, and resumed duty the next day.

The Driver of No 80 Down, Whitemoor- Frodingham goods train also received injury to his nose, and was sent to the local Hospital for treatment. He was not detained there.
Name of this man not known.

Driver Skipworth, Louth Loco. received cuts on the face, but these were not serious.

Members of the staff of all departments were quickly on the scene to render First Aid, and clear up the debris. Some help in clearing up the debris was also given by the Military Authorities.
Had it not been for the fact that the raider machine gunned the town there would have been many more casualties from flying glass and splinters. But at the sound of the Machine Gunning members of the staff quickly took what cover was available.

From 6.0.pm. to 10. 0. pm no passengers travelled past the delayed action bomb, but goods and empty stock trains were run. The passengers were taken by Motor Bus between Louth and Ludboro from down trains rejoining the train at the latter station, similarly on up trains passengers were taken by bus from Ludboro to Louth rejoining the train at Louth. Buses hired from the Lincolnshire Road Car Company.
The site of the delayed action bomb was visited by Mr Orchard of the Engineers Dept, Boston and it was decided that no bomb was there, After this normal working on the down line was resumed.

Members of the Military Bomb Disposal Squad visited the station on Thursday Feb 20th, and after examination etc decided that there was adelayed action bomb on the station. In consequence of this all traffic at the North End of the station was stopped, at 4.50.pm.
Shunting in the goods yard was suspended, and passenger trains terminated at Louth (Down Trains) and Ludboro (Up Trains).
Buses were hired to convey passengers between Louth and Ludboro, an emergency goods service is in operation, goods from the south terminating at Aby, and from the North at Ludboro, being conveyed from these points to Louth by our Motor Lorries. Members of our staff being sent to these points to assist in dealing with the traffic.
This arrangement is still in operation.

that the exploding bomb had caused a severe nose bleed. When I saw what the damage was I told Percy to hold the loose flesh in position, painful as it was, and I set off at a gallop in the direction of the Louth Goods Depot where I knew the First Aid men were to be found. The ambulance men made a first class job, stitching the wound perfectly, so that in later years only a very slight scar showed.

The train had not been damaged too much in the fraças, but the leading van loaded with baby carriages for a Grimsby store was peppered with bullet holes, the nearest only a foot from where I had been crouching. Although the engine was unscarred we were relieved after the raid and travelled home to Grimsby Town station by passenger train, the news of our escapade preceding us via the grape vine. As often happens the story was somewhat mangled by the time we caught up with it. On arrival at Grimsby I was told that I was dead, killed in an air raid at Louth. This twist to the tale was the result of another fireman, G. Bradley of Louth, being killed during the raid in the vicinity of Louth loco.

Without doubt we had been through a most unpleasant experience and although I have had some rough rides on 'K3s', there were none rougher than that winter afternoon in 1941.

Others injured in the raid were porter H.S. Stanley on Louth station, motor driver F. Cope, of Mablethorpe, working in the station yard and engine driver Skipworth of Louth loco. All received first aid treatment from the Louth station ambulance class members before being taken to Louth hospital, none were subsequently detained. 2 H.E. bombs fell directly on the station and exploded.

Severe damage was caused to the guards' room, stores, goods office, ticket collectors' and porters' rooms, the lamp room, ladies waiting room, general waiting room, inspector's office and the booking office. There was also some damage to the station house. The loco shed caught a direct hit causing considerable damage, and blowing a large hole in the side wall of the station arcade. Stock damaged included engine No. 6008, four coaches and a LMS double bolster wagon which was completely wrecked.

Some damage had been done to the down main line between the north end of the station and Keddington road crossing, it was assumed that a delayed action bomb had fallen there and as a result the down main line traffic was stopped and single line working over the up main line put into operation. This lasted from 6.10 pm until 10.00 pm, at which time it was decided that no bomb had fallen there after all and normal service was resumed. The decision was made after a visit by Mr Orchard of the Boston LNER Engineering Dept.

However, on Thursday 20th February, a bomb disposal group from the Royal Engineers examined the site and found that, in fact, there was a bomb. Once again traffic was halted until the bomb had been dealt with, buses took over the passenger traffic and lorries dealt with the goods.

Chapter Fourteen
Signalling

In the early years of railway working semaphore signals controlled the movement of British trains. Signals were usually operated by levers at the foot of the post but in some cases were connected by wires to a group of levers. This gradually led to the erection of signal huts and later raised signal boxes. The reverse motion of the signal arm from its position at 'clear', to horizontal, was affected by a counterweight on a lever pivoted on the signal post. In darkness a white light indicated 'clear', red, 'danger' and green, 'caution'.

The GNR learned much from other companies' experiences. Fixed signals at stations were usually mounted on the opposite sides of the same post. They showed three positions, horizontal for 'danger', lowered to 45 degrees for 'caution', and the arm dropped vertically, inside the slotted signal post, indicating 'clear'. Auxiliary (later 'distant') signals were set up 400 or 600 yards in rear of fixed signals and repeated their instructions. In the early days signalling equipment was supplied and erected for the GNR by Stevens and Son, of Darlington Works. In a contract dated December 1851 they agreed to maintain all signals, lamps and wires etc. for 8d. per signal per week. Later Stevens had some very keen competition from Saxby & Farmer and McKenzie & Holland.

An accident at Abbots Ripton, in 1876, was directly responsible for the GNR adopting the centrally balanced signal arm, known as a 'somersault' signal. The arm now hung clear of the post, in view, rather than disappearing into its slot in the signal post, as before. The signals had two positions only, 'danger' and 'clear', the latter indicated by the arm being in the vertical position. New pattern spectacles were fitted, and on tall posts these spectacles were sometimes fitted in a lower position than the signal arms. In January 1878, the spectacles were fitted with green glass, green taking the place of white to indicate 'clear'. Petrol lamps for illuminating the signals were invented by a GNR employee, John Thomas, and soon replaced the old Brydone candle lamp.

The East Lincolnshire had to wait for re-signalling and the block system, which was not completed to Grimsby until 1884. Two features stand out as regards signalling on the ELR. The first was the particular lever frame, a 4½ inch tappet type, some of which lasted up to the closure. The other was the early practice of having the block instruments inside the (ground level) signal huts, and the lever frames outside. Examples that I am aware of were at Bellwater, before the opening of the New Line, Lade Bank, which remained as such up to closure, and Hainton Street, until 1924, and this despite being disapproved of in the 1890 Board of Trade inspection. Boston High Street, also had an outside frame until the new Goods South Junction box was erected opposite.

Until the closures of 1970, the lines in Lincolnshire possessed a particularly unchanging atmosphere, due in large part to the survival of outwardly unaltered signalling equipment and stations, but also because money was

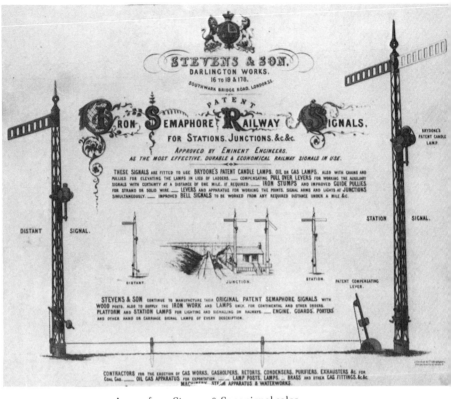

A page from Stevens & Sons signal sales manual.

Early semaphore signals used on the East Lincolnshire Railway.

Stevens' pattern signal with fixed lamp and moving spectacle plate, fitted with a single red glass which cleared the lens when the arm fell into the post.

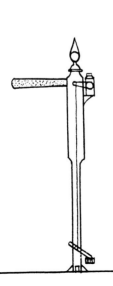

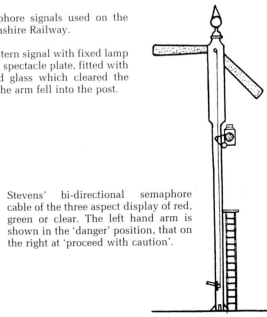

Stevens' bi-directional semaphore cable of the three aspect display of red, green or clear. The left hand arm is shown in the 'danger' position, that on the right at 'proceed with caution'.

tight in an area where local passenger traffic, at best, remained static, and excursion and goods traffic declined steadily from the mid-1950s onwards. At Bellwater Junction, surely the loneliest signal box on the GNR, the New Line joined the ELR, the next station at the time of closure being Firsby, Little Steeping having fallen a victim to the Beeching era elimination of intermediate stations on main lines. This incidentally leads to the present day anomaly where the surviving Grantham to Skegness trains serve rural stations between Grantham and Boston, and then run on a stationless railway for 17 miles until reaching Thorpe Culvert, on the one time Skegness branch, along which the traditional stops are made.

Firsby was a mixture of ancient and modern. The station with its overall roof and classical exterior had changed little by 1970. The signalling arrangements, with the East Junction remotely worked from Firsby Station box in conjunction with continuous track circuiting from Thorpe Culvert were modern. Firsby East Junction box closed in 1927 and was used as a battery house for rows and rows of leclanche cells needed to work the track circuits and the point motors, a duty it fulfilled until a few years before the closure. The logical step of a continuation of track circuiting to Little Steeping in order to eliminate the South Junction box was never completed. There were three somersault bracket signals at Firsby, all different in construction. At the South Junction the down home signals with the Station and East distants were wooden arms on a lattice structure. At the East Junction, the home signals from Skegness with the South Junction distant were corrugated metal arms on an all concrete structure. The third bracket was the home signal at Firsby station from the Skegness direction providing route indications to the down main and bay. This was an unusual late example of all-wooden construction believed to date from 1925.

The north end of Boston station was controlled by a small cabin to the north of the up platform until 1892, when a new box named Grand Sluice was opened near the Witham railway bridge. A 35 lever McKenzie and Holland frame was installed here, later extended to 36 levers when a gate wheel was installed; this box replaced an earlier small box on the same site. On 16th February, 1892 the new box took over the work of the old East Junction box. Grand Sluice box, had no outside steps, access was from a stairway underneath the cabin. The box was closed on 11th November, 1985 and designated a grade 2 listed building.

At Maude Foster box, the first block post on the ELR north of Boston, there survived into the 1970s what must have been the last example of the tall GNR somersault signal, with the arm raised high for a good sky background and the lamp and spectacle assembly positioned lower down the post. Here there was no telephone to High Ferry, the next block post to the north, the single needle telegraph being the only means of communication.

No chapter discussing signalling on the ELR would be complete without mention of William Armitage, of the Fish-shambles, Louth. The *Railway Record* of December, 1848, makes mention of Mr Armitage's achievements:

> We have had our attention drawn to a paragraph which has been going round the daily papers relative to the recent introduction of detonating signals on the North Western Railway, but as that company are not the originators of this mode of giving

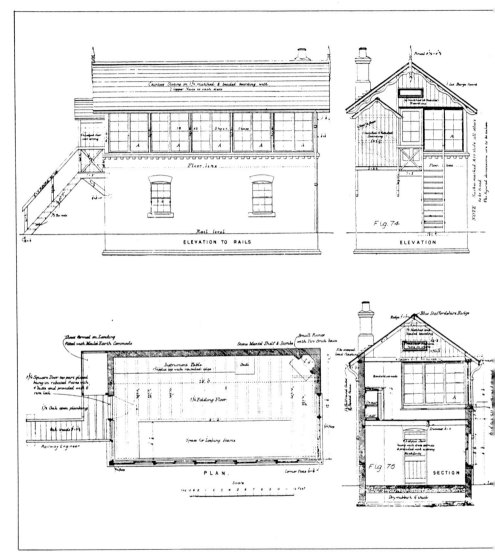

A brick signal cabin (Great Northern Railway) with variations, most signal boxes along the East Lincolnshire line were based on this principle.

notice of any casualties that may exist on the line to imperil the progress of the train, but merely copyists without acknowledging the authorship we think it is due to the loco manager of the GNR to award to him the credit of their introduction, and to Wm Armitage, chemist, of Louth, the inventor of the detonating light, the merit, after much perseverance and labour, of their perfection and certainty of discharge in all states of the atmosphere.

On 22nd February, 1848, what was described as a 'self-illuminating signal', was tried out on the ELR with complete success. It comprised a simple apparatus secured with a strip of lead to the rail, which produced a red light for some minutes when an engine passed over it. The experiments were witnessed by Richard Johnson, the ELR's locomotive engineer.

On 7th September of the same year, as the evening train from Alford was leaving Legbourne, Mr Armitage and Mr Johnson stationed themselves on the line about two miles distant from the station. As soon as Mr Johnson had ascertained that the train was in motion one of Mr Armitage's new red light signals was fired in order to test its efficiency. The signal being immediately recognised, the steam was shut-off and the brakes applied, the train crept cautiously forward for two miles until it reached the experimentors. By this time Armitage was already supplying the GNR with his detonators.

One of Mr Armitage's detonating signals was tried out near Lincoln on 28th October, it was fixed to the rails and as the train passed over it the signal produced a thunderous noise that was heard over a great distance and certainly by the crew of the engine. The experiment was regarded as a success, the signal an effective warning to enginemen of any approaching danger.

It was the detonating signal and its success and popularity with the GNR that caused what the press described as, 'an awful catastrophe – a direful event', which brought about the death of Mr Armitage and four of his household. Behind Mr Armitage's shop, in a courtyard, was an apartment raised on posts and made almost completely of glass which was used by him for taking daguerotype likenessess, at which practice he had become remarkably expert. Close by the house at the rear of the shop was a small studio and joined to that the kitchen with above it the 'Tincture Room'. The two sides of the courtyard were joined across the back by a general warehouse, two storeys in height, which housed drugs etc. It was William Armitage's great skill as a chemist that led to his inventing and manufacturing, 'railway detonating alarm fog signals'. The manufacture of signals took place in the warehouse and tincture room, they were dried in the kitchen.

On Saturday, 17th November, at 2.50 pm, a tremendous explosion wrecked the studio, kitchen, tincture room and part of the warehouse, detonating signals continuing to explode amongst the wreckage. When the acrid smoke had subsided sufficiently to allow an inspection of the wreckage, the bodies of William Armitage, aged 35, Thomas Armitage, his father, aged 60, Kitza Wilson, the housekeeper, aged 26, Mary Evans, 15 and her brother, Stephen, aged 14, assistants in the manufacture of railway signals, were discovered.

The process of making the signals involved the making up of a paste in the warehouse which was then put in tin boxes and placed in an oven to dry. Once dry they were varnished and the lids put on; Stephen Evans then did the varnishing, and his sister carried them in her apron to Mr Armitage who put the lids on. The drying was carried out in the kitchen oven which accounted for the death of Kitza Wilson, who was ironing in the kitchen at the time of the explosion. It appears that the increasing orders from the GNR had necessitated decreasing the drying time and, in consequence, increasing the temperature in the oven, and this, according to the ensuing enquiry into the accident, was the direct cause of the tragic explosion.

The Skegness Bay starting signal at Firsby. A late (1925) example of all-wooden construction. No. 36 is off for a train to depart on the up line for Lincoln, photographed in September 1968.   *G. H. Brown*

Firsby South Junction. These wer wooden arms on a lattice structure. Thi photo shows them minus the finials on 28t March, 1967.   *H. B. Priestle*

Chapter Fifteen
Closure

There were two inquiries into BR's closure proposals conducted by the Transport Users' Consultative Committee (TUCC). The first took place at Skegness in September 1964, when BR proposed closing the whole system north of Boston including the branches to Skegness, Mablethorpe and Coningsby Junction. The hearing lasted for two days and apart from scores of protesting authorities, bodies and individuals the committee received 1,714 written objections, many of them incorporating thousands of separate objections. Perhaps the most stunning comment at that hearing was made by a parish council's representative who pointed out that if the line was to close it would take longer to travel from New York, Lincolnshire, to London than from New York, America, to the Metropolis! Of that inquiry it was reported, 'The lines can be saved only if overwhelming hardship would be caused by their closure. After the meeting there could have been little doubt that such hardship would be caused to thousands of people, that the entire region would be isolated and that economic disaster for the coast would follow.'

In the event the Minister asked BR to look at its proposals again. It did, and in due course once again proposed closure as before, this time excepting the line to Skegness. To these new proposals there were 1,588 objections and the TUCC held another inquiry, again at Skegness, this time in May 1968, lasting two days.

The case for the objectors was opened by Mr Peter Tapsell, MP for Horncastle, who with Mr Richard Body, MP for Holland with Boston and Sir Cyril Osborne and later Mr Jeffrey Archer, MPs for Louth, had fought long and hard for the retention of services. But all was to no avail and on 19th December, 1969 the *Louth Standard* reported,

One of the most ill-conceived Christmas shocks imaginable has been hurled at East Lincolnshire by British Railways and the Government. It is learned that the line between Grimsby and Peterborough is to close, apart from a short stretch giving a link with Skegness via Firsby. There will no passenger service between Boston and Alford and Louth and Grimsby.

BR contended that the local services on the Peterborough to Boston, Firsby to Grimsby and Willoughby to Mablethorpe lines were losing £172,000 a year. The Ministry of Transport's decision to allow the services to be closed stated that the Minister had noted the TUCC's view that closure would cause 'widespread hardship', because of lengthened journey times and increased fares. On the other hand he noted that the great majority of journeys were of an occasional nature and a large proportion of all travellers would in any case be.provided for by other rail services. Of those who used the Grimsby to Peterborough services about one fifth consisted of through travellers between Grimsby and London, and for these there would be an improved service via Newark, with little difference in fares and travelling time. For travel north of Firsby the existing bus services, supplemented as proposed by the railway, partly to provide connections with trains at Market Rasen for Louth and Alford people, would provide acceptable alternatives for all but a very small number. Closure was originally scheduled for the early part of May but it was postponed because there was no time to make arrangements for extra bus services.

The line closed on Monday 5th October, 1970, the last train, a special run by the *Lincolnshire Standard* newspaper ran on Saturday 3rd October. The train left Grimsby for London at 11.10 am, a few minutes after the last scheduled through train powered by class '47', No. 1577, picking up passengers at North Thoresby, Louth, Alford, Burgh, Firsby, Boston and Spalding. Carrying 678 passengers it arrived at Kings Cross several minutes behind the 2.40 pm arrival time. On the return journey it left Kings Cross at 6.57 pm, several minutes before the scheduled train. Between Sandy and Huntingdon it switched to the slow line so that the timetabled train could overtake it and thus make it the last train over the East Lincolnshire line.

On both the outward and inward journeys people gathered at stations, at level crossings and at the lineside to wave farewell to the train. It was on the return journey that the sadness was felt. At each stop the train crew, Mr L. Hodgkinson and Mr P.J. North, of Immingham depot, hastily signed autographs on anything that was thrust at them. At Alford local buglers sounded the 'Last Post', but the biggest demonstration of the day was mounted at Louth where nearly 1,000 people lined the platform five deep as the train drew in at 10.00 pm.

Looking back it seems that the decision to close the line was taken in the 1963 Beeching Report and that the two inquiries at Skegness were merely delaying the inevitable. Certainly the signs were there in 1964, when the *Standard* reported,

> Creeping up the Peterborough to Grimsby line are 'Beeching's death-men', the demolition contractors. They have completed the demolition of Sibsey station. On the platforms busy with passengers until 1961, stood a dragline ripping up the cobbled surface. Yellow painted bulldozers shuffled around the yard dragging down green railings, excavators have torn up the sidings and levelled disused ballast. This is the last of their jobs on the Spalding to Firsby section. They have not yet received the 'all clear' to dismantle the sidings at Eastville and Little Steeping; although the sidings at Eastville may not come up the platforms will certainly come down. At Old Leake the station has already disappeared without trace. Already on the north of the line, Grainsby halt has gone without a sign to show it ever existed. Only piles of gravel remain where platforms were at Utterby, Fotherby and Holton Village.

Always the fundamental issue of reducing operating costs were sidetracked. There were 63 crossings between Grimsby and Peakirk which could have been automated. Heavy traffic was rerouted and freight contracts altered, as though the object was to show that the line could not be an economic possibility. Indeed not long before the closure Louth station was completely rewired, no doubt adding to the unprofitability bill.

The point made by the Ministry that the majority of journeys were of an occasional nature and that a large proportion of passengers would be provided for by other rail services was ludicrous, the inference being that because journeys were not regular no service should be offered. Perhaps of more importance was the fact that the alternative services were totally inadequate. The main weakness of BR's proposals was their inability to recognise the value of the ELR as a useful means of passenger communication within as well as outside the area. Seen in a present day context the ELR was a logical link between London and an expanding Humberside which could have included a rail link across the new Humber bridge (another wasted opportunity).

With the closure of the ELR, the section between Boston and Firsby became part of the Skegness branch; it has survived and continues to create its own history. The section between Louth and Grimsby remained open for another ten years as a freight-only line, its activities well described by Malcolm Roughley who made a journey down the line in the spring of 1980.

I made the aquaintance of Inspector Frank White, from the Doncaster Division, who was to be my guide for the day. We waited for a short time on the up platform of Grimsby Town station, until the arrival of a light locomotive, No. 31113, which had run in from Immingham depot, soon we were trundling back along the main line to Marsh Junction Sidings, to pick up our train for the day.

Marsh Junction forms a triangle on the outskirts of Grimsby, the northern apex of which leads away to Immingham Docks and the locomotive depot there. The line ultimately comes full circle to join the New Holland line, thus providing a kind of lengthy run-round facility with access to the main Grimsby line at Habrough and Brocklesby. Marsh Sidings now provide six or so roads and represent a mere shadow of their former importance; indeed, they are the only BR sidings in the area, as the Immingham complex is owned and operated by the Dock Authority. Our train consisted of a single Vanfit loaded with glass fibre, and a brake van. Promptly at 9.00 am, we left the yard and returned to Grimsby, through the Town station, and took the old GN line at Garden Street Junction.

We were now on the branch proper, and after we had negotiated the double-track curve to Hainton Street signal cabin, which is manned when the trains run, we took the train staff for Louth, and the line became single and stretched away before us like an arrow.

There is a branch speed restriction of 35 mph, but due to the numerous crossings on the line, our actual speed rarely exceeded 15 mph. For the first few years after the line was re-classified as a freight branch, the trip working was operated by an '08' shunter from Grimsby Docks depot, but it was found that the lightly-powered locomotive was unable to cope with exceptional loads, and now the duty is nearly always performed by a class '31'. The service is scheduled to operate thrice weekly, on a Monday, Wednesday and Friday, but as is usual on such lines, the train really runs 'when required'.

It had been some time since the passage of the previous train and the rails were noticeably rusty, although the track seemed to be in good shape. There are no intermediate stations open for traffic or loops en route, and the line is virtually dead straight from Hainton Street to Louth. After three miles we approached the station and gates at Waltham, the second of eight crossing places which are manually operated by the guard. As is the case with most of the station buildings still extant on the line, the structures have been converted into private dwellings, but with the Great Northern flavour still apparent. The platforms too for the most part are still in situ, being of the staggered variety, a feature common to many Lincolnshire wayside stations.

We passed on sedately through the typical Lincolnshire countryside and the flat, cultivated farm-lands, and occasionally attracted the attention of low-flying air-craft. We repeated the crossing-gate manoeuvres at Holton (5 miles), Grainsby (6 miles), North Thoresby (7 miles), Ludborough (8½ miles), Utterby (9¼ miles), and Fotherby (11¼ miles) before approaching the curve which heralds the entrance to Louth.

Ninety minutes running time had brought us to the small agricultural town, some 14 miles from Grimsby, and as Louth North signal box appeared in sight it became clear that the station and surrounds were in a very dilapidated condition: the once-thriving railway community had disintegrated to a mere shell. The station is no longer connected with the branch and, although the main structure has a preservation order placed upon it, the general appearance is one of decay and ruin. Thousands of clerical documents, and slips of paper littered the floor of the vandalised signalling and telegraph offices which are situated opposite the station and hidden almost behind a mass of brambles and overgrown foliage. The engine shed has been demolished some years since; and although the large goods depot was still standing, demolition work on that had already begun.

The remaining signal box, Louth North, is completely inoperative save to work the double gates that span the road and to house a telephone link with the 'outside world'. The long double track approach to the gates is now in effect a run-round facility, guarded only by a defunct shunting signal. A spur runs through the gates and into a siding which serves the giant maltings, which tower high over the whole scene. Close by there is a small freight and parcels office occupied by the solitary BR representative in Louth.

As I wandered round to the front of the station to admire the elegant facade, I was quite unnerved at the thought of how, historically speaking, in the space of a few years, the rise and fall of the railway heritage in this small town was virtually complete.

My reflections were brought to an abrupt halt by a long blast on the locomotive horn. No. 31113 had despatched its wagon with ease and was eager to return home. We returned through the gates and, after attaching the brake-van from the short headshunt, we slowly pulled away into the rain and mist which had rapidly descended. The tall, gaunt gables of the station, standing erect and isolated, receded gradually into the distance, their future theoretically if not practically secure. Our booked departure time of 11.08 had been strictly adhered to, which amused me a little, and our arrival at Grimsby Town Station by 12.50 was right on schedule. I alighted from 31113 and watched the little train amble away to Marsh Sidings.

The line was finally closed at the end of 1980. There was an almost indecent haste about the way BR set about lifting the track during the early months of 1981. The trackbed was designated 'a quarry' by the contractor responsible for removing the ballast and this was despatched with the same rapidity as the track. The only section left *in situ* and that only for a brief while, was the older bullhead section between Grimsby and Waltham distant signal, ironically the very section earmarked by Humberside County Council for their Peakes Parkway feeder road into Grimsby.

Prior to closure a number of people from the Grimsby and Louth areas formed the Grimsby–Louth Railway Group, with the intention of trying to persuade BR and the local authorities to keep the line open. They ran a couple of very successful railtours from Louth, to York and the Keighley and Worth Valley Railway, but it became apparent their efforts were to no avail. This group formed the nucleus of the Grimsby–Louth Railway Preservation Society, formed in 1980 with the intention of opening the whole line between the two towns. Negotiations with BR have continued ever since but look like reaching some sort of conclusion during 1991. The company controlling the preservation society have applied for a Light Railway Order and the society have a tenuous presence on the line at Ludborough, the proposed base for this ambitious project.

Less speculative is the future of Louth station building. This architectural gem certainly deserved better treatment than it received between closure of the line and an application to demolish it, made on 27th March, 1987. It is a tribute to its remarkable construction that it survived at all, its interior being wrecked by vandals, the ball finials pushed off the main entrance and window frames wrenched from their sockets. The lack of effective local action taken to curb or prevent the desecration is extraordinary in a town so well endowed with beautiful architecture; perhaps that itself is the reason for such a philistine attitude. That the demolition application was rejected is justice indeed. The building stands, albeit in a modified form, as a testament to a time when one in five Ludensians worked for the railway, and a reminder to an ungrateful town of the debt it owes to the railways, which brought so much growth and prosperity to the area.

Firsby station signal box on 4th August, 1964. Signalman Moore is pulling off the starting signal. In this box the signalman worked with his back to the lines.

G. H. Brown

Appendix One
Locomotive allocations

Great Northern Railway   December 1922

BOSTON

Class*	Type	Numbers
E1	2−4−0	753/5/8,855,994/5/8/9,1061/4/8
D1	4−4−0	45,1367/71/9/80/2/4/94/5
D2	"	1356/8/60
D3	"	1343/50/7/9
J5	0−6−0	191/5,832/45,1032/83,1106/45
J21	"	13/4/5,73
J22	"	571/2/82/95/9,600/2/4/33/4
C2	4−4−2T	1504/9/10/18
G1	0−4−4T	943
J15	0−6−0ST	153A/92,781/8,856,907
J16	"	620,790

LOUTH

Class*	Type	Numbers
E1	2−4−0	814,1000A
D1	4−4−0	1383
D3	"	1304
C2	4−4−2T	1503/6/13

*GNR classifications

London and North Eastern Railway   March 1933

BOSTON

Class†	Type	Numbers
C2	4−4−2	3987
C12	4−4−2T	4502/4/37
D2	4−4−0	3045,4335/6/80/4/94/5
D3	"	4308/11/43/51/6−60, 4080
J1	0−6−0	3013−5
J2	"	3072−4
J4	"	4083,4106/45
J6	"	3522/49/55/94/5/6/8,3600/4/8/23/33/4
J68	0−6−0T	7029/31/2 Great Eastern Railway
J69	"	7190, 7349/85 Great Eastern Railway
N5	0−6−2T	5547, 5937 Great Central Railway

LOUTH   (Spring 1934)

Class†	Type	Numbers
D2	4−4−0	4369/82/3/97
D3	"	4072,4314/43
C12	4−4−2T	4015,4513/25
J11	0−6−0	6008 Great Central Railway

All ex-GNR engines unless otherwise stated
†LNER classifications

British Railways   1950

BOSTON (Shed Code 40F, closed 1964)

Class†	Type	Numbers
K2	2-6-0	61725/31/44/50/55/56/60/62/70
D2	4-4-0	62154/81
C4	4-4-2T	62900/1
J3	0-6-0	64115/32/37
J6	"	64180/1/90/96/98,201/29/42/44/47/48/76
J2	"	65016/7/20
C12	4-4-2T	67350
Y3	0-4-0T	68166S,171
J69	0-6-0T	68528/43/60/81
J68	"	68655/57/58/59
N5	0-6-2T	69256/61/80
A5	4-6-2T	69808/19

LOUTH (Shed Code 40C, closed 1956)

Class†	Type	Numbers
D3	4-4-0	62132
J11	0-6-0	64320/8
C12	4-4-2T	67352/64/79/81/83/84/98
N5	0-6-T	69306

When the shed closed in 1956 the three remaining locos, Nos. 64320, 64328 and 67398 were moved to Immingham.
†LNER classifications.

With Boston station in the background, GNR class 'G2' locomotive No. 1003 heads north for the East Lincolnshire line in the early 1900s.
P. W. Pilcher Collection, National Railway Museum

Appendix Two
Ivor Smith's observations at Alford Station – April 1934

Date	Time	Type	No. Vehs.	Type of Engine	Remarks
Friday 6/4/34	am 8.57	D.P.	9	Ex GNR class 'C1' No. 4413	
	10.02	U.ExP.	6	Ex GNR class 'C1' No. 4417	
	10.30	D.G.	20	Ex-GNR class 'J1' No. 3015	2 Detached
	10.38	U.P.	3	Ex-GNR class 'D3' No. 4307	
	10.39	D.G. (class 'B')	52	Ex-GCR class 'O4' No. 6624	Frodingham. 10 ton LMS Banana Van, 6 wheel brake (15 tons) fitted, 2 plate wagons, fitted open wagon, built by NBL Atlas Works. 1919, No. 22225.
	10.45	D.L.	3	Ex-GCR class 'O4' No. 6571 No. 6518 No. 5153	1. Frodingham NBL. 1917 in steam: 2. Frodingham. NBL. 'dead'. 3. Frodingham Kitson, Leeds. 1914 'dead'
	12.00	U.G. Class B	22	Ex-GNR class 'D3' No. 4080	Horse box. Ventilated. Refrigerated.
	pm 12.05	U.Tm White-moor	24	Ex-GCR class 'O4' No. 6182	22 Hoppers, full. 2 × 4 wheel brakes.
	12.40	U.T.	13	Ex-GNR class 'J1' No. 3532	
	1.07	U.P.	9	Ex-GNR class 'D3' No. 4383	Horse box.
	1.22	U.ExP.	14	Ex-GNR class 'C1' No. 4413	1 × 8 wheel fish van.

Date	Time	Type	No. Vehs.	Type of Engine	Remarks
Friday 6/4/34 continued	1.30	U.Tm.	—	Ex-GCR class 'O4' No. 5377	2 plate wagons.
	2.20	D.E.F.	46	Ex-GNR class 'K3' No. 206	6 wheel brake.
	3.05	U.L.	—	Ex GNR class 'K3' No. 80	
	3.57	U.P.	12	Ex-GCR class 'D9' No. 6027	4 fish, Brake No. 455, 3 oxfits.
	4.07	D.P.	6	Ex-GNR class 'C1' No. 3291	Brakes. 496, 41289.
	4.14	U.G.	30	Ex-GNR class 'J6' No. 3634	12 cattle, 4 wheel brake.
	4.30	D.G.	41	Ex-GNR class 'D3' No. 4307	1 Detached, 23 Attached.
	4.59	D.E.F.	61	Ex-GNR class 'K3' No. 180	4 wheel brake. Ferryhill (fitted).
	6.05	U.P.	6	Ex-GNR class 'D3' No. 4383	2 fish.
	6.58	D.Ex.P.	8	Ex-GCR class 'D9' No. 6027	
	7.45	D.P.	6	Ex-GNR class 'D3' No. 4359	
Saturday 7/4/34	am 6.44	U.P.	6	Ex-GNR class 'D3' No. 4369	
	8.57	D.P.	6	Ex-GNR class 'C1' No. 4413	Brake No. 4189.

Date	Time	Type	No. Vehs.	Type of Engine	Remarks
Saturday 7/4/34 continued	10.02	U.Ex.P.	8	Ex-GNR class 'C1' No. 4417	
	10.25	Thro' D.G. 'B'	66	Ex-GCR class 'O4' No. 5377	17 Hoppers, 9 plate wagons, Plough brake (Southern Area).
	10.30	D.G. 'B'	19	Ex-GNR class 'D3' No. 4080	1 NER, Sleeper (10 Tons).
	10.38	U.P.	4	Ex-GNR class 'D3' No. 4307	Horse Box, Louth to Mumby Road.
	11.30	U.G.	20	Ex-GNR class 'J1' No. 3015	6 wagons fly shunted. NE Container, 20 ton fitted 6 wheel brake.
	11.53	U.Ex.P.	8	Ex-GCR class 'B2' No. 5423	Sir Sam Fay Restaurant car.
	pm 1.07	D.P.	12	Ex-GNR class 'D3' No. 4369	Corridor.
	1.22	U.Ex.P.	14	Ex-GNR class 'C1' No. 4413	
	2.20	D.E.F.	40	Ex-GNR class 'K3' No. 125	6 wheel brake.
	2.25	U.L.	—	Ex-GNR class 'K3' No. 180	
	3.05	U.Tm.	69	Ex-GCR class 'O4' No. 5005	
	3.57	U.P.	6	Ex-GCR class 'D9' No. 6029	Milk Van.
	4.07	D.P.	7	clas 'J39' No. 1270	Brakes, 4129, 413.

Date	Time	Type	No. Vehs.	Type of Engine	Remarks
Saturday 7/4/34 continued	4.10	U.G. 'B'	48	Ex-GNR class 'J3' No. 3555	4 wheel 10 ton brake, 14 cattle wagons.
—	—	D.G.	49	Ex-GNR class 'D3' No. 4307	20 attached, 4 detached, 2 LMS, 4 NE. 4 wheel brake, LMS oxfit.
Sunday 8/4/34	pm 1.20	D.Ex.P.	11	Ex-GNR class 'C1' No. 3289	
	4.21	D.P.	7	Ex-GNR class '2' No. 3254	1 refrigerated.
	7.31	U.Ex.P.	15	Ex-GNR class 'C1' No. 3289	10 miles in 8½ minutes, dead stop, lamp out.

KEY:
U = Up; D = Down; Ex = Express; P = Passenger; F = Fish; G = Goods; Tm = Tarmac;
L = Light Locomotive(s); E = Empty.

An Immingham based class 'K3' locomotive No 61842 at Boston in April 1951. The 'K3s' were used extensively on the Grimsby fish traffic over the East Lincolnshire line. What a pity one of these powerful engines was not preserved.   *P. R. Batty*

Appendix Three
Staff at Louth Station, 1920s and 1930s

Frank Gooding, who worked at Louth between 1927 and 1934, and after that at Alford, recalled the names of Louth personnel during that period.

Station Masters: Messrs Ireland, Bruntlett, Mitchell and Johnson
Station Master's Clerk: John Baggley
Inspectors: Ernie Buckett and George Pickard
Chief Booking Clerk: George Crosby
Clerks: Fred Crosby, Randall Lancaster, Les Ness and George Faulkner
Ticket Collectors: Alf Pickering, Bert Snowden and Fred Ranger
Porters: Bob Hewins, Alf Wright, Sam Tomkinson, Charlie Wallace, Sep Stanley, Freddie King and Harold Brant
Lads: Frank Gooding, Ernie Parrott and Wilf Copping
Goods Shed Foreman: Mr Trexworth followed by Bill Handley
Checker: Tom Page
Chief Clerk: J. Luck; *Deputy Chief Clerk:* P. Spencer, W. White
Goods Messenger: Jack Richardson
Weighbridge: Jim Bellamy
Goods Shunters: T. Hodson, Harold Thompson, C.A. Marshall and Ron Bellamy
Horse Delivery Driver: Fred Good, Bill Lawston and Bill Wade
Shunt Horse Drivers: Billy Bourne, Frank Mitchell and Jim Green (relief)
Signalmen: Walt Clark, Charlie Hammond and George Gice (South Box); Freddie Parsons, Harry Brant, George Hodson, Arthur Mabelson (North Box)
Rlf Signalmen: Mr Murfin, George Hammond and Frank Greenfield
Running Foreman: Mr Cheetham
Enginemen: Messrs Cartwright, Tuxworth, Janney, Smalley, Welbourne, Sands Paddison, Smith, Ingoldmells, Appleby and Cox
Guards: Messrs Gooding, Willey, Burgess, Cant, Summer, Holden, Claricoats, Creek, Royle, Stow, Bolton, Atkin, Newham
S&T Linemen: Frank Sutton, Bill Stanley and Tom Ayre
Signal Fitter: Horace Parker

Louth also had two inspectors, Mr Parrott who was responsible for the main line and Mr Coupland responsible for the Bardney and Mablethorpe branches.

Apart from it being a tribute to Frank Gooding's remarkable memory, the list gives a good idea of the size of the operation at Louth in terms of manpower. It is also nice to be able to recognise the efforts of all ranks; the names of station masters are usually listed in Directories, not so, horse shunters.

References and Acknowledgements

Deposited plans, maps and Ordnance Survey maps in the possession of Lincoln City Library
The Lincolnshire Archives
Grimsby Reference Library and private sources
The Lincoln, Rutland and Stamford Mercury
The Lincolnshire Chronicle
The Illustrated London News
The Lincolnshire Standard

The History of the Great Northern Railway by C.H. Grinling (Methuen, 1898)
The Great Northern Railway, 3 volumes, by John Wrottesley (Batsford, 1979)
Great Northern Steam by W.A. Tuplin (Ian Allan, 1971)
Great Northern Locomotive History, 3 volumes, by N. Groves (R.C.T.S.)
Locomotives of the LNER parts 3A, 3B, 5, 6A and 7 (R.C.T.S.)
A Bibliography of British Railway History by G. Ottley (Allen & Unwin, 1965)
LNER Constituent Signalling by A.A. MacLean (OPC 1983)
The Engineer, The Great Northern Railway Supplement, 1913
The Railways Around Grimsby, Cleethorpes and Immingham by P.K. King and D.R. Hewins (Foxline, 1988)
Lincolnshire Potato Railways by S. Squires (Oakwood Press, 1987)
On the Line (G.L.R.P.S.)
The Louth to Bardney Branch by A.J. Ludlam and W.B. Herbert (Oakwood Press, 1987)
The Louth, Mablethorpe and Willoughby Loop by A.J. Ludlam (Oakwood Press, 1987)
The Gresley Observer, various.
Boston a Railway Town two parts by Adam Cartwright & Stephen Walker (KMS 1987)

Special thanks are due to the staff of the Lincoln City Reference Library for their unstinting help, also Lincolnshire Library Services, Louth; The Grimsby College of Technology and Arts Library; The National Railway Museum; The Great Northern Railway Society; Public Record Office, Kew; The Gresley Society.

Individuals who have helped include Michael Back, George Bullock, Adam Cartwright, Philip Crome, Godfrey Croughton, Dick Dunnett, John Edgington, Tony Evans, Brian and Pam Gooderham, Frank Gooding, Geoff Goslin, Peter Holmes, Colin Judge, Paul King, Kenneth Leech, Eric Neve, Bob Riddington, Malcolm Roughley, Mrs Ivor Smith, Alan Turner and many others.

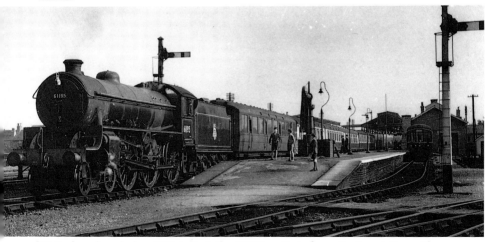

Immingham based class 'B1' 4—6—0 No. 61195 waits to leave Boston station with the 4.58 pm Peterborough to Firsby service on 30th June, 1956.   *H. B. Priestley*

Index

*and train workings